Emma's Nauvoo

EDITED BY RONALD E. ROMIG

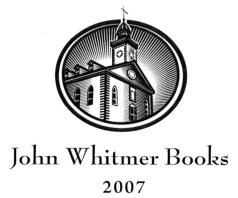

John Whitmer Books
2007

For Emma

Emma's Nauvoo
Edited by Ronald E. Romig
Copyedited by Rene Romig and Lavina Fielding Anderson

John Whitmer Books
Independence, Missouri
JohnWhitmerBooks.com

Published in the United States of America
Second printing with corrections
ISBN 978-1-934901-03-8

Copyright © 2007 by Ronald E. Romig
18 Oak Hill Cluster, Independence, Missouri 64057
rromig1@comcast.net

Without limiting the rights under copyright reserved above, no part of this publication may be reproduced, stored in or introduced into a retrieval system, or transmitted, in any form or by any means (electronic, mechanical, photocopying, recording, or otherwise), without the prior written permission of the publisher.

Images, unless otherwise cited, are the copyrighted intellectual property and provided courtesy of Community of Christ Archives, 1001 W. Walnut, Independence, Missouri 64050-3562.

Cover and interior design by John Hamer
Typesetting by Ronald E. Romig

FRONT COVER IMAGE: David H. Smith, painting of the bend on the Mississippi River, ca. 1868. Left to right: David H. Smith, the painter, Rosalind Newberry, or Tryphenia Hall, possibly Julia Murdock Smith, David's sister, or his cousin Emma Smith, and his mother Emma Smith Bidamon. Image used by permission of the Community of Christ Archives and the Lynn Smith Family.

BACK COVER IMAGE: Engraving of Nauvoo Temple Ruins, James Lindforth, ed., *Liverpool to Great Salt Lake City*, illustrated by Frederick Piercy (Liverpool, England: Franklin D. Richards, 1855), between pages 62 and 63.

Table of Contents

Brief Biography of Emma Hale Smith Bidamon	1
A Nauvoo Setting, Hostile Neighbors, Visiting the Mansion House	6
Lucy's Mummies, Egyptian Mummies advertisement	7
Maps of Nauvoo and vicinity	8
Photographs of Emma	9
Emma on Her Own	10
Nauvoo Mansion Rental, Agreement between Emma and William Marks	11
Red Brick Store Rental	12
Emma's Image, ca. 1850s	13
Joseph's New Translation of the Holy Scriptures	14
John Bernhisel Letter to Emma Smith, William Marks's Contract Expires	13
Almon Babbit, Joseph Smith III Regarding George Edmunds	16
Mormon Exodus, 1846	17
Mr. Van Tuyl, Manion House Rental, *Warsaw Signal*	18
Emma's Situation, Emma and Brigham Young	19
Brigham Young Jr. Statement, 1867	20
Battle of Nauvoo, Thomas L. Kane	21
John Scott, 1848, Temple Fire	26
A Place for Emma's Family, Henry Lewis, 1848	27
From New Orleans to Nauvoo, James Ririe, 1853	28
Visits to the Mansion House, Sessions, 1852, Eldredge, 1853	29
James Quayle, 1853	30
Lucy Mack Smith, William McLellin, 1840s	31
Hannah King, 1853, Frederick Piercy, 1853	32
Enoch Tripp, 1855, Lucy Mack Smith's Death	34
Emma's Family Through the Years, Joseph Smith III, Enoch Tripp	35
Edmund C. Briggs, 1856	36

Joseph F. Smith's Reminiscence of a Visit to Nauvoo, 1860	43
Nancy J. Tharpe, 1869	45
Recollections of Nauvoo, Julius Chambers, 1872	46
William McLellin's Visit, 1847	49
Portraits of Joseph and Emma, Front View Oil Portrait	50
Portrait Location, Samuel H. B. Smith	51
Charles Debault Portrait of Joseph, Junius Wells's Visit	52
George F. A. Spiller, 1856	53
Emma Smith Bidamon Letter to Emma Pilgrim, 1870	54
Joseph Smith's Revision of the Holy Scriptures	56
Tribute to Emma, 1866, Emma to Joseph III, 1867	57
Joseph III's Presidency of the RLDS Church and Polygamy	58
E. C. Briggs, William McLellin	59
William McLellin, 1861, Joseph Smith III to A. W. Dennetts, 1876	60
Joseph Smith III Letter to J. J. Barbour, 1878, Emma's Illness	61
Joseph Smith III Letter to James Cobb, 1879	62
Emma's Last Testimony, 1879	64
The Interview with Emma	65
Emma's Passing, Alexander H. Smith	70
Emma's Obituaries	73
Reflections of Emma, Emma's Burial	80
David S. Holmes Reminiscence, 1915	81
Lou Hudson, James Jimison, Statements, 1940	82
Louis C. Bidamon's Passing, 1891	84
Inez Smith Davis, 1930	86
Smith Family Burial Ground	88
Resources about Emma	90
Afterword, Joseph Crawford Poem, 1879	92

Emma's Nauvoo

Brief Biography of Emma Hale Smith Bidamon

EMMA HALE (1804-79), was born 10 July 1804, in the Susquehanna Valley in Harmony Township (present-day Oakland), Pennsylvania, to Isaac Hale and Elizabeth Lewis Hale. Unlike many other young women of her day, Emma received one year of extra schooling beyond the common grammar school education. She matured soon into a stately, handsome, and dark-haired young woman.

Emma Hale Smith Bidamon - holding David Hyrum Smith, ca. 1845

Emma met Joseph Smith when he was working with his father near Harmony, Pennsylvania, employed by Josiah Stowell, an acquaintance of the Hale family. Their relationship blossomed quickly, and the couple married on 18 January 1827 in South Bainbridge, New York. She was twenty-two years old. Emma explained to her son, Joseph III, "My folks were bitterly opposed to him; and, being importuned by your father . . . who urged me to marry him, and preferring to marry him to any other man I knew, I consented." The newlyweds moved to Manchester, New York, to make their home with Joseph's parents.

In the fall of 1827, Emma accompanied Joseph to Hill Cumorah where they obtained the Book of Mormon plates. The couple returned to Emma's parents in Harmony to work on a translation of the plates. Joseph bought a piece of land from his father-in-law. On 15 June 1828, Emma gave birth to their first child, a boy, who died within a few hours. Early in June 1829, Emma and Joseph moved to the Peter Whitmer Sr. home in Fayette, New York. By the end of

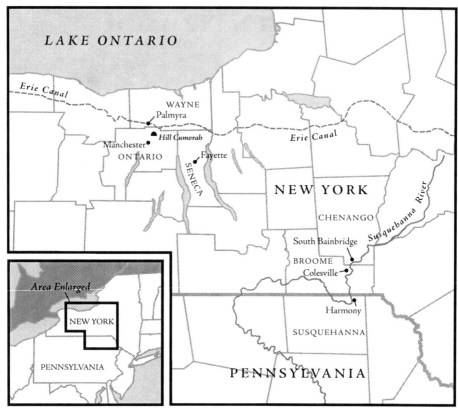

Sites in the early married life of Joseph and Emma Smith. Map courtesy of John Hamer.

June the translation was completed. The Book of Mormon was published in Palmyra, New York, and ready to distribute during March 1830.

Joseph Smith and a small group of his followers organized the Church of Christ, on 6 April 1830. Emma was baptized a member of the new church at Colesville, New York, on 28 June and confirmed in August 1830. While in the Harmony area, in July 1830, Joseph called Emma by revelation "to expound Scriptures, and to exhort the church," to act as scribe, encourage her husband, and select hymns for use by the church.

In January 1831, Joseph and Emma moved to Kirtland, Ohio, the newly appointed church headquarters. In late April of that year, Emma gave birth to twins. Both of the babies died within a matter of hours. Soon after, Joseph and Emma adopted the motherless newborn Murdock twins, Joseph and Julia.

On 24 March 1832, Emma watched as her husband was dragged from the John Johnson house and tarred and feathered by an angry mob. Her adopted son, Joseph, died five days later from exposure to the cold.

Emma continued to support her husband's efforts during the construction of the Kirtland Temple by inviting builders into her home for hot meals and places to rest. With William W. Phelps's help, Emma produced a hymnal which was used during the dedication of the Kirtland Temple in March 1836. Two more sons, Joseph (later known as Joseph III), born 6 November 1832, and Frederick Granger Williams, born 20 June 1836, were added to the family. Both Joseph and Frederick lived to manhood.

Sites in Emma's life. Map courtesy of John Hamer.

In 1838, Emma followed her husband and other members of the church to Far West, Missouri. There, Emma gave birth to another son, Alexander Hale, on 2 June 1838. When the church was expelled from the state of Missouri by order of the governor, Emma left her husband behind in state custody. With two babies in her arms and two more children clinging to her skirts, she crossed the frozen Mississippi on foot in search of refuge in Quincy, Illinois. She also carried the manuscript of her husband's new translation of the Bible hidden in pockets under her clothing.

Joseph escaped from his Missouri jailors and rejoined his family in Illinois. Joseph soon designated Nauvoo, Illinois, as the new church headquarters. Emma and Joseph moved into a small log house known as the Homestead, located near the river. She would remain in Nauvoo until her death in 1879.

Emma gave birth to three more sons in the coming years, losing one at birth and a second at eighteen months to a fever.

In 1842, the Smith family began moving from the Homestead across the street to the Nauvoo Mansion.

Later that year, Emma was elected president of the Female Relief Society of Nauvoo. Under Emma's direction, the society sought to fortify community morals and relieve the poor. The organization grew from twenty women to more than 1,100 its first year.

As early as 1840 Joseph Smith began introducing a secret religious ordinance to some of his associates known as the endowment. Emma eventually became the first woman to receive an endowment and later officiated as other women participated in this ceremony.

After Joseph's death on 27 June 1844, Emma chose not to participate in any more temple ordinances. A final child, David Hyrum, was born 17 November 1844.

Following Joseph's death, Emma actively resisted the practice of plural marriage and the

The Homestead, 1890s.

leadership of Brigham Young. Her first priority became the preservation of an inheritance for her five living children. However, distinguishing Joseph's personal property from that of the church was no easy task. This issue threw Emma and Brigham Young into a series of complex and often bitter legal entanglements.

When Brigham Young led a large portion of church members to the Rocky Mountains in 1846, Emma elected to remain in Nauvoo with her family. On 23 December 1847, Emma Smith married Major Lewis Bidamon, a non-Mormon, further separating her from former friends. She was devoted to her mother-in-law and cared for Lucy Mack Smith until Lucy's death in 1856.

Emma Smith Bidamon's final years in Nauvoo were family-focused and private. Major Lewis Bidamon assisted Emma in raising her five children and was her companion until her death in 1879 in Nauvoo.

—Based on Carol Cornwall Madsen, "Emma Hale Smith," *Encyclopedia of Mormonism*, 3:1321-26.

Front left: Lewis Bidamon, Frederick G. W. Smith, Joseph Smith III.
Back left: David Hyrum Smith, Alexander. H. Smith.

A Nauvoo Setting

Thomas C. Sharp, *Warsaw Signal* editor.

Hostile Neighbors

FOLLOWING THE death of Joseph Smith, Thomas C. Sharp, the editor of the *Warsaw Signal*, in neighboring Warsaw, Illinois, used his press to keep anti-Mormon sentiment stirred up. Sharp called for further action against the Mormons, writing, "Now it is evident there can be no peace in Hancock, while there is a vestige of Mormonism left. The hostility of the two parties towards each other is such that there never can be a reconciliation...."
—*Warsaw Signal*, 7 January 1846.

Visiting the Nauvoo Mansion House

EUDOCIA MARSH recorded an interesting description of the Smith Mansion House. Eudocia grew up outside of Carthage, Illinois, and visited Nauvoo on an outing with some of her family members late in 1843 or in 1844, prior to Joseph Smith's passing. She was about fifteen at the time.

Her group ... dined at the Mansion House Smiths [sic] large Hotel. After dinner we were told that in an adjoining room some Egyptian Mummies were exhibited for a small sum—

Some of the party expressing a wish to see them, we found them presided over by the mother of the Prophet, a trim looking old lady in black silk gown and a white cap and kerchief.
—Eudocia Baldwin Marsh, "Mormons in Hancock County, A Reminiscence," *Journal of the Illinois State Historical Society*, 64, no. 1 (Spring 1971):38.

Lucy's Mummies

Lucy Mack Smith, ca. 1845-50.

IN 1834, Joseph Smith Jr. had acquired a collection of ancient Egyptian scrolls and mummies from a travelling curiosity peddler. The scrolls formed the basis of his BOOK OF ABRAHAM, but the mummies were put in the charge of his mother, Lucy Mack Smith, who exhibited them to visitors for a small fee.

Detail from scroll found with mummies.

EGYPTIAN MUMMIES,

Lately imported into this country from
ALEXANDRIA
in

EGYPT

And opened for the first time in New York, in the presence of some of the most respected physicians & citizens.

These Mummies have been exhibited in Philadelphia, and at the Baltimore Museum, to large audiences.

Of all the relics of the Ancient world that time has left, the Mummy is decidedly one of the most interesting. All other Antiquities are but the works of man, but the Mummies present us with the men themselves. An hundred generations have passed away since this flesh was animated, since these eyes were bright and this tongue was eloquent.

ADMISSION 25 cents

Advertisement for what became Lucy Mack Smith's mummies from the *Lancaster (Pennsylvania) Journal*, ca. 1834.

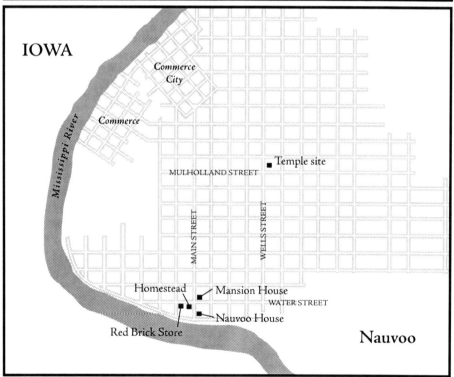

Nauvoo and its vicinity. Maps courtesy of John Hamer.

EMMA'S NAUVOO

Photographs of Emma

These photographs were all taken after 1870 and depict Emma in the later years of her life. During the 1870s access to photography had become quite commonplace.

Emma *On* Her Own

William Marks, ca. 1850

AFTER JOSEPH SMITH Jr.'s death, Brigham Young and his supporters informed Emma that Joseph's property belonged to the church. Emma resisted their efforts to control Joseph's estate. Instead, to provide for her children, she took measures to consolidate family lands and property holdings. Though some church members and former friends treated Emma unkindly during this period, other individuals who had been friends with Joseph provided encouragement and support.

Prompted by the need for money for expenses associated with the settlement of Joseph's estate, Emma entered into an agreement with William Marks, former Nauvoo Stake president. Marks took possession of the Nauvoo Mansion Hotel and operated the facility for one year. Emma reserved several rooms in the building for her family's use.

Nauvoo Mansion House, ca. 1843, Nauvoo, Illinois.

Nauvoo Mansion Rental

Article of Agreement Between Emma Smith and William Marks

THIS ARTICLE of agreement made and entered into this 25th day of Aug. A.D. 1844 between Emma Smith of the County of Hancock and State of Illinois of the one part and William Marks of the County and State aforesaid of the other part.

Witnesseth that the said Emma Smith hereby agrees to rent to the said William Marks the following described property to wit The house Comonly called the Nauvo Mansion situated on lot NA 3 Block NA 147 in the City of Nauvoo and also said lot.

And also the Barn and Barn lot situated on lot No one Block No 156 togeather with all appertaining thereunto or in anywise belonging to the same in consideration of which the said Wm. Marks hereby Binds himself in the penal sum of four hundred dollars to pay as an anual [sic] rent the sum of two hundred dollars, and further more the said Wm. Marks agrees to let the said Emma Smith keep a horse and Carriage in said Barn and also to keep the premises in as good repair as when the said Wm. Marks takes possesion and he is to have possesion on the first day of Sept. A. D. 1844 and to hold the same for one year.

In testimony whereof the said parties have hereunto set there [sic] hands and seals the day and year above written.

Done in presence of :
Emma Smith [Seal Symbol]
Joseph W. Coolidge
William Marks [Seal Symbol]

[On back of document:]
Nauvoo March 4th 1845
Received on the within Leace or bond two hundred Doolars being the full amount of rent.
Emma Smith
[Original spelling retained.]

—Emma Smith, article of agreement with William Marks, 25 August 1844, Emma Smith Papers, P4, f26, Community of Christ Archives.

Red Brick Store Rental

AS A SUPPLEMENT to the family's meager income, Emma also attempted to rent out the Red Brick Store. Emma wrote to a former friend, Joseph Heywood, hoping to interest him in renting the store.

Red Brick Store, ca. 1890s, Nauvoo, Illinois

Nauvoo, Oct. 18, 1845

Brother Heywood,

Sir I send by the stage twenty three bags, wishing brother Hollingshead to send some oats by the St. Bt. Osprey as soon as is convenient. The brick store will be emty [sic] next week, and I would like well if you could find it advantageous to your interest to fill it with goods and groceries this fall, the rent will be low.

I think it a good time to commence an establishment of that kind here now as there is a number of the merchants about to leave here soon.

My family are all in good health at present, and the brethren are generaly [sic] well with the exception of Amasa Lyman who has been very sick but is better now.

My best respects to your family and all our friends. Tell Sister Heywood I shall keep those shoes she gave to Mr. Smith as a memento [sic] both of her and my husband too, for I can never see them with [out] remembering them both.

Respectfully your most obedient Emma Smith

Mr. J Heywood

—Emma Smith Bidamon letter to Mr. J. Heywood, 18 October 1845, Emma Smith Papers, P4, f27, Community of Christ Archives.

Red Brick Store for rent, 1845.

AROUND 1850, Joseph Smith III was photographed while holding a daguerreotype of his mother Emma.

THIS IMAGE OF EMMA fills in a photographic gap in Emma's life between 1845, when she was photographed holding her young son, David Hyrum Smith, and the early 1870s.

Joseph Smith III, ca. 1850,
Holding a treasured daguerreotype.

Emma Smith Bidamon,
daguerrian image, ca. 1850.

Joseph's New Translation *of the* Holy Scriptures

EVEN WHILE struggling to support her family, Emma devoted attention to matters of long-term importance. The preservation of her husband's manuscript revision of the Holy Scriptures is one of Emma's many accomplishments. She understood the work's value, having assisted her husband by acting as a scribe many years earlier. She later carried the manuscript materials from Missouri to Illinois, crossing the frozen Mississippi River with the compilation hidden under her skirts. Finally, she preserved the revised manuscript after her husband's death.

Joseph continued working on the manuscript throughout the Nauvoo era. He had the manuscript at home upon the occasion of his death. When church authorities asked for it, Emma refused to turn it over. Instead, she kept it in her own possession and eventually allowed her son Joseph III, as president of the Reorganized Church, to publish its contents in 1867.

After Joseph's death, Dr. John M. Bernhisel, a close friend of

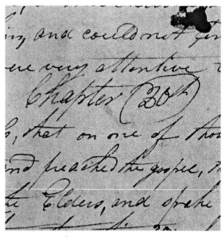
Detail from translation, Luke 20.

Joseph, continued to take an interest in Emma and her family by frequently visiting the family. Upon one such visit, in May 1845, Emma Smith let him review the New Translation manuscripts of the Holy Scriptures. Bernhisel recalled:

> I had great desire to see the New Translation but did not like to ask for it; but one evening, being at Bro. Joseph's house about a year after his death, Sister Emma to my surprise asked me if I would not like to see it. I answered, yes. She handed it to me the next day, and I kept it in my custody about three months. She

told me it was not prepared for the press, as Joseph had designed to go through it again. I did not copy all that was translated leaving some few additions and changes that were made in some of the books. But so far as I did copy, I did so as correctly as I could.

— John Bernhisel statement, preserved in L. John Nuttall, "Diary One," 10 September 1879, 335, Perry Special Collections, Brigham Young University, Provo, Utah.

John Bernhisel to Emma Smith

Nauvoo October 9th 1847

DEAR SISTER EMMA, I cannot take my departure from this place, without acknoledging [sic] the debt of gratitude that I am under to you. And in making this acknowledgment, I especially desire to be understood that I am observing no mere form or idle custom, nor empty ceremony. During the three years that I was a member of your family, I found every necessary provided for my comfort, with much order and neatness, and from yourself and family, I experienced not only kindness and respect, but such affectionate regard, tenderness and delicacy as to make me feel more than your grateful friend.

I may never be permitted to pay you all, but the bond of obligation shall ever remain binding on my heart and life. And I beg you to accept my profound and grateful acknowledgments for your uniform kindness and attention to me, and for your trouble of me during so long a period; and I fervently pray that God may reward you in this world a thousand fold, and in the world to come with life everlasting.

J. M. Bernhisel

—John M. Bernhisel, letter to Emma Smith, 9 October 1847, Emma Smith Papers, P4, f29, Community of Christ Archives.

WILLIAM MARKS'S contract on the Nauvoo Mansion expired in 1845. Emma's status as a young widow with a family was precarious. The situation in Nauvoo was growing more desperate, as non-member violence towards the Mormons rapidly increased.

Brigham Young and others of the Twelve Apostles planned to lead the church away from Nauvoo into the great American West.

But even amidst their preparations for departure, some in the church still planned to institute legal proceedings that would interfere with Emma's control of Joseph Smith's estate.

During this time of transition, the family came to see Brigham Young as their primary antagonist. In their minds, Brigham represented all that was unsavory about Mormonism.

Almon Babbitt

Church agent Almon Babbitt, wrote the following about the Smith Estate in later years:

THERE WERE TWO later episodes concerning the estate. First, one of the creditors, Phineas Kimball, obtained a state-court judgment against the estate in March 1852 for about $5,000. To satisfy the debt, several properties held by Joseph Smith, Jr. in a personal capacity were ordered sold. L. C. and Emma Smith Bidamon were able to retain the Nauvoo Mansion, the Nauvoo House, and other properties only by bidding for them at the auction, June 5, 1852.

Second, in 1856, twelve years after her husband's murder, Emma was able to secure part of the dower money which the federal government erroneously had neglected to pay her. This was accomplished by a special act of Congress, providing a payment of $197.35.

—Almon Babbitt, "What Do I Remember of Nauvoo?" 339; see Oaks and Bentley, *Joseph Smith and Legal Process*, 779-80, notes 186, 188; also Tullidge, 770.

ON 28 March 1910, Joseph Smith III wrote a letter to his son, Israel A. Smith, recalling Judge George Edmunds's role in rescuing the family during this legal process:

"I have the sincerest regard and respect for Judge Edmunds, for it was through his unflinching regard for the right, and a sincere respect for mother and her family, that we saved anything of much value out of father's estate, as a combination of which one Phineas Kimball was the center would have robbed us, if Judge Edmunds had not stood in the way."

—P13, f1035, Community of Christ Archives.

Mormon Exodus, 1846

ON 4 FEBRUARY 1846, the Mormons began crossing the Mississippi River by ferry. Soon the river froze solid, opening the way for an accelerated exodus. On 16 February 1846, families and wagons lined up for miles at Parley Street waiting their turn to cross the frozen river. Along with their wagons, livestock, and personal belongings, several thousand church members had soon reached the other bank, leaving behind them Nauvoo, the "City Beautiful."

Anti-Mormon forces pressured any remaining church members to exit the city as quickly as possible, hoping to take possession of the now-abandoned valuable properties.

WARSAW SIGNAL.

Th. Gregg--Editor and Publisher.   The Past--the Present--for the Future.   One Dollar a Year in Advance.

THOUGH EMMA did not plan to follow church members west, she felt it would be safest to take her family away from Nauvoo for a time. Emma recalled:

A Mr. Van Tuyl had offered to rent the Mansion from me, so I decided that I would accept his offer.... I rented the Mansion completely furnished; bedding, dishes, cookware... everything.

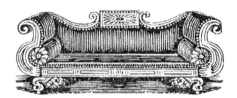

EMMA completed her business in Nauvoo and moved to Fulton, Illinois. Before long, a neighbor contacted her, warning that Van Tuyl was leaving without notice and taking Emma's dishes, bedding, and furniture with him.

Rumors of Van Tuyl's suspicious behavior spread up and down the river.

The *Warsaw Signal* printed the following inquiry and notice:

THE MANSION HOUSE, NAUVOO.—
[Despite rumors] we have heard this popular Hotel lightly spoken of, by some of our citizens, and its obliging and accommodating host—Dr. Abram Van Tuyl—recommended to the traveling public. Will our friends who visit Nauvoo, call on the Doctor and see "if these things are so?"

—*Warsaw Signal*, Vol. 3, No. 14 (July 1, 1846).

EMMA returned to Nauvoo by steamer, while neighbors detained Van Tuyl. Fortunately, she caught him red handed. He left town, but without Emma's belongings.

—Erwin E. Wirkus, *Judge Me Dear Reader: Emma Smith Tells Her Own Story as Seen by Wirkus* (Las Vegas, Nevada: Ensign Publishers, 1978), 33.

Emma's Situation

THE DIARIES AND journals of many former church members and other travelers who passed through Nauvoo offer brief glimpses into the circumstances of Emma's Nauvoo.

In July 1847 J. H. Buckingham called on Emma at the Nauvoo Mansion:

> We found her at home and had considerable conversation with her. She is an intelligent woman, apparently about fifty years of age, rather large and good looking with bright sparkling eyes but a countenance of sadness when she is not talking. She must have been a handsome woman when some years younger.
>
> —Buckingham, *Boston Courier*, July and August 1847, reprinted in the *Herald*, 101 (15 March 1954):251.

Emma *and* Brigham

Brigham Young, ca. 1865

BRIGHAM YOUNG JR. reflects his father's displeasure with Emma after Joseph Smith Jr.'s death in the following memorandum, which was written in 1867. [There appears to be no basis for Young's claim that Emma wrongly obtained Hyrum Smith's painting. Hyrum's family took his portrait to Utah. It is now at BYU.]

Item Respecting Emma Smith, 1867.

[On Latter-day Saints' European Printing Publishing and Emigration Office Letterhead.]
42 Islington, Liverpool
April 1st, 1867.

ITEMS RESPECTING the property and money given by the Church to Emma Smith previous to the expulsion of the Saints from Nauvoo.

H. C. Kimball obtained from Ellis M. Saunders fifteen hundred dol. to liquidate debts contracted by Joseph Smith, but when bro Kimball arrived at Nauvoo and found that the prophet had been assassinated, he gave the money to Emma Smith: Afterwards She de<nied> ever having received Such an amount of money from bro K. but he pos<e>sed [possessed] indubitable proof of the fact.

The Cleaveland Farm, 4 miles out of Quincy, a very valuable property was deeded to Emma Smith by the Trustee in Trust before leaving Nauvoo.

The farm <320 acres> lying two miles out of Nauvoo, near the burying ground, was deeded to Emma by the advice of the Twelve.

Just before Joseph['s] death, he deeded over the White purchase which consisted of about two hundred acres of ground on which a part of Nauvoo was built.

Did not Emma Smith go to Mary, Hiram [Hyrum] Smith's widow, and take possession of a valuable portrait of Hiram, and <keep it> despite the tears and supplications of the widow, to again be put in possession of the portrait of her husband? And did she not then and there demand to be shown a valuable <gold> ring which belonged to Hiram—similar to one Joseph had, and put <it> in her pocket and refused to return it to the rightful owner? Again, she went to the widow of Don Carlos Smith, and by misrepresentation succeeded in obtaining possession of another gold ring—similar to Hirams [Hyrum's]—and kept it utterly refusing to restore the property sureptitiously [sic] obtained.
Brigham Young, Jr.

—Items personally obtained from Prests. B.Y. & H.C.K. G.S.L City Feb. 3rd, 1867. Utah Tery. U.S.A. Brigham Young, Jr., re: Emma Smith, 1 April 1867, Photostat, Emma Smith Papers, P4, f38, Community of Christ Archives.

Battle of NAUVOO

BY SPRING 1846 THE majority of the Mormons had left Nauvoo, but still a large number remained. On 11 September 1847, the "Battle of Nauvoo" broke out. The city was cannonaded. After a week of artillery shelling, the Mormons abandoned Nauvoo entirely. In the process much property was destroyed. What remained of Nauvoo was occupied by newcomers.

A very detailed description of post-Mormon Nauvoo was outlined by Thomas L. Kane. Kane later became a great friend of the Mormons and assisted with their migration westward.

Thomas L. Kane

A FEW YEARS AGO, ascending the upper Mississippi in the Autumn, when its waters were low, I was compelled to travel by land past the region of the Rapids....

I was descending the last hillside upon my journey, when a landscape in delightful contrast broke upon my view. Half encircled by a bend of the river, a beautiful city lay glittering in the fresh morning sun; its bright new dwellings, set in cool green gardens, ranging up around a stately domed-shaped hill, which was crowned by a noble edifice, whose high tapering spire was radiant with white and Gold. The city appeared to cover several miles; and beyond it, in the back ground, there rolled off a fair country, chequered by the careful lines of fruitful husbandry. The unmistakable marks of industry, enterprise and educated wealth, everywhere, made the scene one of singular and most striking beauty.

It was a natural impulse to visit this inviting region. I procured a skiff, and rowing across the river, landed at the chief wharf of the city. No one met me there. I looked, and saw no one. I could hear no one move; though the quiet everywhere was such that I heard the flies buzz, and the water-ripples break against the shallow of the beach. I walked through the solitary streets. The town lay as in a dream, under some deadening spell of loneliness, from which I almost feared to wake it. For plainly it had not slept long.

There was no grass growing up in the paved ways. Rains had not entirely washed away the prints of dusty footsteps.

Yet I went about unchecked. I went into empty workshops, rope-walks and smithies. The spinner's wheel was idle; the carpenter had gone from his work-bench and shavings, his unfinished sash and casing. Fresh bark was in the tanner's vat, and the fresh-chopped lightwood stood piled against the baker's oven. The Blacksmith's shop was cold; but his coal heap and ladling pool and crooked water horn were all there, as if he had just gone off for a holiday. No work people anywhere looked to know my errand. If I went into the gardens, clinking the wicket-latch loudly after me, to pull the marigolds, heart's-ease and lady-slippers, and draw a drink with the water sodden well-bucket

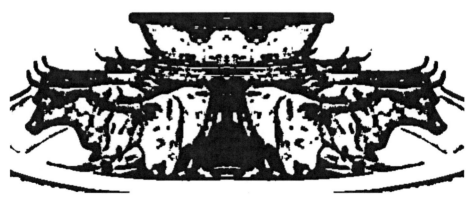

Nauvoo Temple, Baptismal Font, Twelve Oxen

Thomas L. Kane

and its noisy chain; or, knocking off with my stick the tall heavy-headed dahlias and sunflowers, hunted over the beds for cucumbers and love-apples,—no one called out to me from any opened window, or dog sprang forward to bark an alarm. I could have supposed the people hidden in the houses, but the doors were unfastened; and when at last I timidly entered them, I found dead ashes white upon the hearths, and had to tread a tiptoe, as if walking down the aisle of a country church, to avoid rousing irreverent echoes from the naked floors.

On the outskirts of the town was the city graveyard. But there was no record of plague there, nor did it in anywise differ much from other Protestant American cemeteries. Some of the mounds were not long sodded; some of the stones were newly set, their dates recent, and their black inscriptions glossy in the mason's hardly dried lettering ink. Beyond the grave-yard, out in the fields, I saw, on one spot hard-by where the fruited boughs of a young orchard had been roughly torn down, and still smoldering embers of a barbecue fire, that had been constructed of rails from the fencing round it. It was the latest sign of life there. Fields upon fields of heavy-headed yellow grain lay rotting ungathered upon the ground. No one was at hand to take in their rich harvest. As far as the eye could reach, they stretched away–they, sleeping too in the hazy air of Autumn.

Only two portions of the city seemed to suggest the import of this mysterious solitude. On the southern suburb, the houses looking out upon the country showed, by their splintered woodwork and walls battered to the foundation, that they had lately been the mark of a destructive cannonade. And in and around the splendid Temple, which had been the chief object of my admiration, armed men were barracked, surrounded by their stacks of musketry and pieces of heavy ordinance. These challenged me to render an account of myself, and why I had the temerity to cross the water without a written permit from a leader of their band.

Though these men were generally more or less under the influence of ardent spirits; after I had explained myself as a passing stranger, they seemed anxious to gain my good opinion. They told me the story of the dead city: that it had been a notable manufacturing and commercial mart, sheltering over 20,000 persons; that they had waged war with its inhabitants for several years, and had been finally successful only a few days before my visit, in an action fought in front of the ruined suburb; after which, they had driven them forth at the point of the sword. The defense, they said, had been obstinate, but gave way on the third day's bombardment. They boasted greatly of their prowess, especially in this Battle, as they called it . . .

They also conducted me inside the massive sculptured walls of the curious Temple, in which they said the banished inhabitants were accustomed to celebrate the mystic rites of an unhallowed worship. They particularly pointed out to me certain features of the building, which, having been the peculiar objects of a former superstitious regard, they had as a matter of duty sedulously defiled and defaced. The reputed sites of certain shrines they had thus particularly noticed, and various sheltered chambers, in one of which was a deep well, constructed they believed with a dreadful design.

Beside these, they led me to see a large and deep chiselled marble vase or basin, supported upon twelve oxen, also of marble, and of the size of life, of which they told some romantic stories. They said, the deluded persons, most of whom were immigrants from a great distance, believed their Deity countenanced their reception here of a baptism of regeneration, as proxies for whomsoever they held in warm affection in the countries from which they had come: That here parents "went into the water" for their lost children, children for their parents, widows for their spouses, and young persons for their lovers: That thus the Great Vase came to be for them associated with all dear and distant memories, and was therefore the object, of all others in the building, to which they attached the greatest degree of idolatrous affection. On this account, the victors had so diligently desecrated it, as to render the apartment in which it was contained too noisome to abide in.

They permitted me also to ascend into the steeple, to see where it had been lighting-struck on the Sabbath before; and to look out, east and south, on wasted farms like those I had seen near the city, extending till they were lost in the distance....

It was after nightfall, when I was ready to cross the river on my return. The wind had freshened since the sunset; and the water beating roughly into my little boat, I headed higher up the stream than the point I had left in the morning, and landed where a faint glimmering light invited me to steer.

Here, among the dock and rushes, sheltered only by the darkness, without roof between them and the sky, I came upon a crowd of several hundred human creatures, whom my movements roused from uneasy slumber upon the ground.

Passing these on my way to the light, I found it came from a tallow candle in a paper funnel-shade, such as is used by street venders of apples and peanuts, and which flaring and uttering away in the bleak air off the water, shone flickeringly on the emaciate features of a man in the last stage of a bilious remittent fever....

Dreadful, indeed, was the suffering of these forsaken beings. Crowded and cramped by cold and sunburn, alternating as each weary day and night dragged on, they were, almost all of them, the crippled victims of disease. They were there because they had no homes, nor hospital, nor poor-house, nor friends to offer them any. They could not satisfy the feeble craving of their sick: they had not bread to quiet the fractious hunger cries of their children. Mothers and babes, daughters and grandparents, all of them alike, were bivouacked in tatters, wanting even covering to comfort those whom the sick shiver of fever was searching to the marrow.

These were Mormons, famishing, in Lee county, Iowa, in the fourth week of the month of September, in the year of our Lord 1846. The city,—it was Nauvoo, Illinois....

The party encountered by me at the river shore were the last of the Mormons that left the city....

—Thomas L. Kane, *The Mormons: A Discourse Delivered before the Historical Society of Pennsylvania, March 26, 1850* (Philadelphia: King and Baird, 1850), 4-6.

John Scott, 1848

JOHN SCOTT visited Nauvoo in 1848. While there, Scott climbed onto the roof of the Temple to look over the city and report on the situation.

It's truly a scene of destruction.... All parts of the temple, city and surrounding country is one scene of desolation; horror and dread seemed to be depicted in the countenance of every person that lives in Nauvoo. Not even the saints that lived there are altogether clear of the same doleful looks.

—John Scott, Journal, 28 February 1848, LDS Family and Church Historical Department Archives, cited in Glen Leonard, "Remembering Nauvoo: Historiographical Considerations," *Journal of Mormon History*, 16 (1990): 28.

Temple FIRE!

IN NOVEMBER 1848 AN arsonist set fire to the Nauvoo Temple. Then, in 1850, a tornado virtually destroyed all that remained. The stones were hauled off for use in the construction of new homes and structures.

A Place *for* Emma's Family

FOLLOWING THE Battle of Nauvoo, Emma returned to the Nauvoo Mansion. Emma's family at this time was composed of young Joseph III, 14; Frederick Granger Williams, 10; Alexander Hale, 8; David Hyrum, 2; and Julia Murdock, 15. Emma supported her children by boarding visitors in the Nauvoo Mansion House.

Emma's marriage to Nauvoo resident Major Lewis Crum Bidamon in 1847 provided welcome protection for family and property holdings.

Henry Lewis, 1848

HENRY LEWIS, A traveling painter of views of the Mississippi River, visited Nauvoo. Of Emma he said:

"[Though married to] a man named Bidamon ... is always call'd the widow Smith." Lewis described her as "a remarkably fine looking woman I should judge of some 35 or 40 years of age [she was actually 44] with a strongly mark'd tho' kind and intelligent face on whose surface are the marks of much care and suffering .... [She] supports herself and family by keeping one of the largest and best hotels in the place and seems to be doing a thriving business."

—William Moulder, "Nauvoo Observed," 98, quoting from John Francis McDermottt, "Henry Lewis' Great National Work," *The Lost Panoramas of the Mississippi* (Chicago: University of Chicago Press, 1958), 114, see Henry Lewis, 1848, *Das Illustrirte Mississippihal, The Valley of the Mississippi Illustrated*, Minnesota Historical Society.

Julia Murdock, ca. 1850

STEAMBOAT FROM NEW ORLEANS TO ST. LOUIS, TIME THREE DAYS.

From New Orleans to Nauvoo

Ririe Visit to Emma, 1853

We then took passage up the river on a steamer. We were six days and one night in getting to St. Louis. That day we changed vessels and started for Keokuk. Next night we landed at Keokuk so our sailing was done with. We lay three days at Keokuk and then started for the plains. Such bad roads I have never seen. We went 13 miles from Keokuk and lay over. We lightened up and burnt boxes and goods. I threw away about 100 pounds of clothing, etc.

On Sunday, about twenty of us went across the Mississippi River to Nauvoo. We saw the ruins of the Saints' homes, the ruins of the Temple and we visited the Nauvoo Mansion. We saw Mr. Bidamon, the man who married Emma Smith. We saw Lucy Smith, the Prophet's mother, and also Emma. We also saw his three sons, Joseph, Frederick, and David. David was then in his 9th year and Joseph was 21. We also saw Mr. Bidamon's little girl about the same age as David. They were all playing together about the house.

—James Ririe, 1853.

Visits *to the* Mansion House

Nauvoo Mansion House, 1852

Perrigrine Sessions, 1852

CROST THE Mississippi River to Nauvoo to put up staid to [t]he Mansion house [30 Nov.] saw the Mother of the prophet Joseph was quite feble but recollected me and apered quite glad to see me saw Emma the Prophets wife and his mother she was glad to hear my voice but could not see me Emma seamed to bee verry cool and indifferent and though so well acquainted in days gone by seamed to bee a stranger to me and to that spirit [that] caracturized her and the Prophet when he lived and she has four children but looked as though of atruth they were without a father they once had every thing looked gloomy about the mansion the spirit of God has departed Nauvoo and the home of the Prophet.
—Donna Toland Smart, ed., *Morman Midwife*, 166- 67.

Horace Sunderlin Eldredge

Horace S. Eldredge, stayed at the Mansion House on 28 July 1853. An afternoon stroll around the city afforded:

THE MOST peculiar feelings that ever I had while walking those streets. Contrast with former days of "gayety and pleasure and the Marks of industry and perseverance" by "a once happy people" who followed "principals of eternal truth" from a fallen leader at the hands of "a rough uncouth profane aspirant." Emma was chilly to him. Of Lucy he noted, "The old lady seemed to know me and was verry much pleased to See me, and made many enquiries about Hyrum & Samuel Smiths families who are in the Valley . . . Mother Smith seemed to retain her recollection verry well of things that had transpired several years since. She wished me to remember her to many or all of her friends in the valley."

—Horace S. Eldredge, 1853 Journal, Daughters of Utah Pioneers, Pioneer Memorial Museum, Salt Lack City, Utah.

James Quayle, 1853

THE STEAMBOAT Deavernon took us up the river to Keokuk, where we were to stay for seven weeks until June 1st, waiting for cattle & wagons to cross the plains.

We got there Tue., 12th. Stopped in warehouse that night. 13th Wednesday camped the night for first time, 14th gypsying. Sunday 17th went to meeting at half past 10 o'clock prayer by Elder James Whitworth addressed by Elder Rostchin followed by Jonathan Midgley followed by Elder Cyrus H. Wheelock. Meeting dismissed by E. Spackman. Camped the week following. Sunday April 25th went to meeting. Monday 26th washing day. Tue 27th went to Nauvoo with James Whitworth, John Sheppley, and Charles Kemp. We crossed the Mississippi river in a scow from Iowa's side to Nauvoo, and visited Joseph Smith's store, after which I and James Whitworth went to Nauvoo Mansion to dinner, then occupied by Bidamon, the second husband of Emma Smith, Joseph Smith the prophet's wife. After noon of same day we visited the temple, then in ruins, and places of interest in the city and surrounding country. That night to supper at Nauvoo Mansion and lodged there that night. Wednesday 28th left Nauvoo at 8 A.M. traveled to Carthage and visited the jail where Joseph and Hyrum were murdered. On the way we spoke to Joseph Smith Jun and his brother Alexander three miles from Nauvoo. They were tramping out oats with horses on the barn floor. We arrived at Carthage P.M., 18 miles from Nauvoo. Took supper at the Carthage hotel kept by Mr. C. S. Hamilton, where the bodies of Joseph and Hyrum lay the night after the murder, lodged there night of April 29th. The next morning after breakfast, took stage for the Mississippi, crossed the river and got to camp that night at Keokuk.

Left Keokuk June 1st 1853 with two yoke of oxen and a yoke of cows, with tents and wagons, Cyrus H. Wheelock being our captain.

—James Quayle, 1853; *http://www.isle-of-man.com/ manxnotebook/mormon/jquayle. htm*, accessed 26 December 2006.

Lucy Mack Smith

EMMA CARED FOR Lucy Mack Smith, her mother-in-law, during Lucy's final years. After her son Joseph's death Lucy had remained in Nauvoo in a house on the corner of Hyde and Kimball Streets, which had been given to her by the Council of Twelve. However, Lucy only lived there for several months before the Battle of Nauvoo forced her to flee the city in 1846. For a time, Lucy moved near Galesburg, Knox County, Illinois, where she lived with her daughter Lucy and son-in-lae Arthur Millikin. William B. Smith also made his home nearby. Mother Smith eventually moved back to Nauvoo. She spent her last days living with Emma's family in the Mansion House. Toward the end of her life, Lucy suffered from severe arthritis and spent much of her time in a wheelchair or in bed. Several visitors to Nauvoo mentioned Lucy in their reports.

William McLellin, 1840s

ON OUR WAY [back to Kirtland, Ohio after concluding our business] we called at the city of Nauvoo again, and visited while there, that superb structure, "the Nauvoo Temple." We also visited old mother Smith, and found her very feeble indeed, from age, hardships, exposures, and sorrows. Her faith and confidence in her religion, seemed only to have gathered strength by the varying vicissitudes through which she has passed during a long life. She took great interest in rehearsing maters combined with the death of her sons. I must say that I walked mournfully through the fated city of desolations.

—McLellin, "Our Apology —and Our Tours, *The Ensign of Liberty*, 1, no. 3 (December 1847), 34, 35.

Hannah King, 1853

ON 12 MAY 1853, WHEN British convert Hannah T. King called on the family, Lucy was: "pillowed up in bed" but alert and articulate. She is a splendid old lady, and my heart filled up at sight of her–she blessed us all, "With a Mother's blessing" and bore her testimony to the work of the last days, and to Joseph Smith as a prophet of the Lord . . . . my heart melted for I remembered my own dear mother left in England for the gospel's sake, and the deep fountains of my heart were broken up. . . . Lucy made a great impression on me . . . She is a character that Walter Scott would have loved to portray and he would have done justice to her.

—King, typescript, 136, 178.

Liverpool to Salt Lake

Frederick Piercy, 1853

THE FIRST OBJECTS I saw in approaching the city were the remains of what was once the Temple, situated on the highest eminence of the city, and which, in the days of its prosperity, must have been to it, what the cap or top stone is to a building. On the banks of the river lie broken blocks of stone and shattered bricks, and the visitor's first steps are over evidences of ruin and desolation. Foundations of what must once have been substantial buildings are broken up and exposed to the light, and houses, once noted for neatness, cleanliness and order, and surrounded by flower gardens, evincing taste, care, and a love of the beautiful, after being pillaged of all that was valuable and portable, have been abandoned by their ruthless destroyers, and are now monuments of their selfish, jealous and contemptible hate.

At present the Icarians form the most important part of the population of Nauvoo. I was told while there that they were by no means in a prosperous condition, and M. Cabet had publicly said, that unless they received assistance from France [they were finished] . . . .

Etienne Cabet — Icarians

While in Nauvoo I lodged at the Nauvoo Mansion, formerly the residence of Joseph Smith, and now occupied by his mother, his widow and her family. I could not fail to regard the old lady with great interest. Considering her age and afflictions, she, at that time, retained her faculties to a remarkable degree. She spoke very freely of her sons, and, with tears in her eyes, and every other symptom of earnestness, vindicated their reputations for virtue and truth. During my two visits I was able to take her portrait, and the portraits of two of her grandsons also.

That of Joseph, the eldest son, was done on his 21st birth-day. He was born about 2 o'clock in the morning of the 6th of November, 1832, at Kirtland, Ohio. He is a young man of a most excellent disposition and considerable intelligence.

One prominent trait in his character is his affection for his mother. I particularly noticed that his conduct towards her was always most respectful and attentive. The other portrait is of David, the youngest son, who was born 5 months after the assassination of his father.

He was born about 8 o'clock in the morning of the 17th of November, 1844. He is of a mild, studious disposition, and is passionately fond of drawing, seeming to be never so happy as when he has a pencil and paper in his hand. The other two boys whom I saw, were very fine, strong, healthy fellows, and as it may be interesting to many, I will say, that during some conversation which I had with persons in

Joseph Smith III — by Piercy, 1856

the neighborhood, I found that the whole family had obtained a most excellent reputation for integrity and industry...."
—Frederick Pierey, *Route from Liverpool to Great Salt Lake Valley*, edited by James Lindforth, (Liverpool: Franklin D. Richards, 1855), 63-66.

The ruins of the Nauvoo Temple — by Piercy, 1856.

Enoch Tripp

IN NOVEMBER 1855 Tripp found Lucy Mack Smith "living in a lonely room in the eastern part of the house; she was ... very feeble.... She arose in bed and placing her hands around my neck, kissed me exclaiming, 'I can now die in peace since I have beheld your face from the valleys of the mountains.'"
—Quoted in Linda King Newell and Valeen Tippetts Avery, *Mormon Engima: Emma Hale Smith*, p. 265.

Lucy Mack Smith's Death
14 May 1856

Joseph Smith III Letter to John Bernhisel

GRANDMA DIED THE morning of the 14th of May last easily and with her senses to the last moment and we trust she has no wish to return from the "bourne." She appeared somewhat fearful of death a little while before he came yet appeared resigned afterwards.

I sat by her and held her hand in mine till death relived her–the first death scene I ever witnessed–Long may I be spared the death scene of my mother.

—Joseph Smith III, Letter to John M. Bernhisel, 24 January 1856, MS 370, fd. 4, microfilm of holograph, LDS Church Archives, as quoted in Lavina Fielding Anderson, ed., *Lucy's Book: A Critical Edition of Lucy Mack Smith's Family Memoir* (Salt Lake City, UT: Signature Books, 2001), 796.

Emma's Family
Through *the* Years

Joseph Smith III, 1855

YOU MAY PERHAPS LIKE to learn of the changes time has wrought in the appearance of those who housed with you the winter of '46 and '47, well, I am now 22 and am about 5 feet 8 1/2 inches tall, weigh 178 pounds and am as ugly as folks generally get to be in this country. Fred is nearly if not quite six feet high and very good looking at least the girls all think him handsome. He is 17 in his eighteenth year. Alex is nearly as tall as I am and looks about the same he ever did. But David is the boy of all boys, the pet of the family and the very personification of gentleness and goodness. Mother has grown old though she bears up well. She is just the same kind mother that she always was. Our step father is as good as step fathers can be. He loves us all as well as he does his own children of which he has two, both girls, both married.

—Joseph Smith III, to Emma Knight, 14 April 1855, Miscellaneous Letters and Papers, P13, f102, Community of Christ Archives.

Enoch Tripp Describes Emma's Family

AN ACCOUNT OF LDS Elder Enoch B. Tripp's visit to Nauvoo appears in the entry for the 25 November 1855 in Journal History, an LDS Church chronology. Enoch Tripp visited Nauvoo while returning from a mission and recorded that he found Emma very bitter against Brigham Young. It was his percepton that her children had inherited the same spirit.

Joseph, her oldest son, is a very strong spiritual medium and claims that he through writing (by placing his hands with a pencil on paper) can converse with his father. I informed him that God, angels and the servants of God never have, and never will, converse with the children of men in that way, but that that was the way the powers from beneath communicated with men.

—*Journal History*, 25 November 1855, Enoch B. Tripp, Journal, Perry Special Collections, BYU.

Edmund C. Briggs, ca. 1870s

Edmund C. Briggs
"VISIT TO NAUVOO," 1856

IN THE EVENING WE had some little conversation with his mother [Emma]. She made several inquiries about our meetings and the interests of the church at Zarahemla, and we informed her of the evidence we had received of her son taking the leadership of the church, as it was his right by lineage. She seemed to wish to avoid any reference about her children having anything to do with the church; spoke of her former husband with tears in her eyes.

The next morning she said: "I have always counseled the saints who come to me for advice as to where they should go, to go north."

I inquired, "Why did you give them that counsel? Did you think James J. Strang's claims were right?" She quickly replied, "No, but I thought if they went up north they could soon get away again, but if they went west they could not, and I always believed the church would rise again in the north. I have always avoided talking to my children about having anything to do in the church, for I have suffered so much I have dreaded to have them take any part in it. But have always believed that if God wanted them to do anything in the church, the same One who called their father would make it known to them, and it was not necessary for me to talk to them about it; but I never had confidence in Brigham Young, and Joseph did not for some time before his death."

I then said to her: "Did Joseph have any knowledge or premonition of his death before it took place?" She replied: "Yes, he was expecting it for some time before he was murdered. About the time he wrote those letters that are in the Book of Covenants he was promised if he would go and hide from the church until it was cleansed he should live until he had accomplished his work in the redemption of Zion, and he once left home intending not to return until the church was sifted and thoroughly cleansed; but, his persecutors were stirring up trouble at the time, and his absence provoked some of the brethren to say he had run away, and they called him a coward, and Joseph heard of it, and he then returned, and said, 'I will die before I will be called a coward.' He was going to find a place and then send for the family, but when he came back I felt the worst I ever did in my life, and from that time I looked for him to be killed, and had felt so bad about it, that when he was murdered I was not taken by surprise, and did not feel so bad as I had for months before."

Emma Smith Bidamon, ca. 1870

While she talked to us the tears flowed from her large, bright eyes like rain, and I could see in every act affection for Joseph.

Delineating her evidence of the divine authenticity of the Book of Mormon, she said: "When my husband was translating the Book of Mormon, I wrote a part of it, as he dictated each sentence, word for word, and when he came to proper names he could not pronounce, or long words, he spelled them out, and while I was writing them, if I made any mistake in spelling, he would stop me and correct my spelling, although it was impossible for him to see how I was writing them down at the time. Even the word Sarah he could not pronounce at first, but had to spell it, and I would pronounce it for him.

When he stopped for any purpose at any time he would, when he commenced again, begin where he left off without any hesitation, and one time while he was translating he stopped suddenly, pale as a sheet, and said, 'Emma, did Jerusalem have walls around it?' When I answered 'Yes', he replied, 'Oh! I was afraid I had been deceived.' He had such a limited knowledge of history at that time that he did not even know that Jerusalem was surrounded by walls."

She also spoke very highly of Elder William Marks and said, "Joseph always had confidence in him.

David Whitmer, ca. 1880

David Whitmer is honest, and when you see him you will say he is an honest, truthful man, and the reason he absented himself from the church was because of his misunderstandings, and the acts of some in the church he could not fellowship."

I then referred to Oliver Cowdery and Martin Harris, when she said: "Oliver Cowdery was an honest man, but he became disaffected because of the actions of some in the church." Of Harris: "He was an honest man, but not naturally as noble and firm in his mind as some.

There were only three classes that, followed Brigham Young to Utah: knaves, fools, and those whose circumstances and environments compelled them to go."

Brother Gurley was much pleased with what Joseph and his mother both said, though at first he was greatly disappointed at the way Joseph received what he had

Zenas Gurley Sr., ca. 1880

said, or, as he expressed it, "Would not allow me to say anything." But we were both impressed that he was aware of his calling as the successor of his father, but that human agency would not influence him to take any stand in the church, and that he was unalterably and utterly opposed to polygamy. As Brother Gurley put it, "He gave us to understand he would not go to Utah, and I am glad of that, anyway."

I was really glad in my heart to

see the manner in which he resented what he first thought we wished to urge upon him as the views against his own convictions. We also thought he was impressed with the fact that we were sincere and believed that we were divinely impressed to visit him with our message, and that we would not accept him as the successor and president of the church without he was truly called of God as his father was.

The next day Brother Gurley still felt so badly about leaving home that he could not endure the thought of continuing in the ministry. I urged him to remain in the mission and we would visit as many of the members of the church as we could and tell them of our hope of the reorganization, but his struggles were too great, and the next Wednesday evening he said to me, "Brother Briggs, I am going home to Katie in the morning—if I lose my salvation." I saw there was no use in trying to persuade him to continue longer in the ministry, and after some conversation we had prayer, and in the best of feelings and spirit we talked over our hope, and agreed that he should return home. The next morning he left me in Nauvoo, and went home. It was as I had expected before we left—I was alone . . . . I remained in Nauvoo and vicin-

Frederick Granger Williams Smith, ca. 1860

ity until the fall of '57; worked a part of the time with Joseph on his farm; though he had moved into the city and his brother Frederick worked the place. I became quite well acquainted with the Smith family.

Frederick was prepossessing; in fact, a gentleman in his appearance, open and frank in his countenance, six feet high and well-proportioned, and I noticed he was very affectionate to his mother, and often saluted her with a loving kiss and good morning or good-by. Everybody loved him.

Joseph was always cheerful, very respectful to his mother, always seemed to be busy. Alexander was always quiet around the house and

David H. Smith — by Piercy 1856

doing chores. David was a handsome boy, modest and retiring disposition, studious, and quite an artist; loved and admired by everybody who formed his acquaintance. Sister Emma was an exceptionally good woman whom everybody spoke of as an example worthy of imitation. In fact, the whole family were esteemed by all people who knew them as good, worthy citizens above reproach, having the reputation of being strictly moral and temperate in all things....

The people, in and out of the church, about Nauvoo, who personally knew Joseph Smith before he was murdered, spoke of him with respect, and declared he was a good, honorable man, a worthy citizen, and declared the scandalous stories circulated about him were base misrepresentations put in circulation because of religious intolerance or by his political enemies. At the same time, the newcomers into the city after the death of Smith who spoke against him were rabid in their denunciation of him, and delighted in telling extravagant stories about him, though they had never seen him....

Mr. R. H. Loomis, who was an honorable man and well acquainted with Joseph, said: "I believe Mr. Smith was honest and conscientious in his religion, and did not teach or practice polygamy."

And Sister Emma, in speaking of the condition of the church after her husband's death, said to me, "I was threatened by Brigham Young because I opposed and denounced his measures and would not go west with them. At that time they did not know where they were going themselves, but he told me that he would yet bring me prostrate to his feet. My house was set on fire several times, and one time wood was piled up at the side of the house and set afire. It burned the siding considerably and went out before we discovered it. It was either set on fire or by

accident or carelessness caught fire a number of times and went out of itself when we did not discover it and put it out, but I never had any fear that the house would burn down as long as the Inspired Translation of the Bible was in it. I always felt safe when it was in the house, for I knew it could not be destroyed.

She spoke very affectionately of Joseph and said, "I never had any reason to oppose him, for we were always on the best of terms ourselves, but he allowed some others to persuade him in some measures against his will, and those things I opposed. He was opposed to the destroying of the press of the Nauvoo Expositor, but the council overruled him by vote, and he told them they were the cause of its destruction, but he would be held personally responsible for it; and often heard Joseph contend against measures in council, and sometimes he would yield to them."

I said, "Those were city councils?"

She replied, "Sometimes, and other times in councils of the church, which were often held in our house. For the last eighteen months or two years before his death it seemed the best elders were kept away from him as much as possible on missions, and the worst characters in the church hovered around him all the time.

. . . I was also present when my brother, Jason Briggs, asked Sister Emma in relation to the purported revelation on polygamy published by Orson Pratt in 1852, and she again denied that her husband ever taught polygamy, or that she ever burned any manuscript of a revelation purported to favor polygamy, and that "the statement that

Orson Pratt

I burned the original of the copy Brigham Young claimed to have, is false, and made out of whole cloth, and not true in any particular." My brother was quite particular in his inquiry when she said, "I never saw anything purporting to be a revelation authorizing polygamy until I saw it in the Seer, published by Orson Pratt." Several were present at the time, and I shall never forget the candid manner of her expression when she, without a single hesitancy, with honesty and truthfulness marking her countenance, gave the lie to Brigham Young's assertion on the 29th of August, 1852, in Salt Lake City when he said, "The original of this revelation was burned up . . . Sister Emma burned the original.["] The reason I mention this, is because that the people who did not know of the revelation supposed it was not now in existence."

—Edmund C. Briggs, "Visit to Nauvoo," 1856, *Journal of History*, 9 (October 1916): 452-62.

Alexander H. Smith, ca. 1865

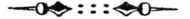

Right: Two of Emma's sons, Alexanter Hale (top), and Joseph Smith III (bottom), as they appeared during the 1860s.

Joseph Smith III, ca. 1860

Joseph F. Smith, Reminiscence of a Visit to Nauvoo, June 1860

Joseph F. Smith, 1866

ON REACHING THE Mississippi River, Joseph F. and Samuel H. B. Smith visited Nauvoo and called upon Emma Smith, who was then the wife of one Major Bidamon. On entering the room where Emma Smith was seated, they were presented to her by her son Frederick G., who said: "Mother, do you know these young men?" She looked up and said: "Why, as I live, it is Joseph. Why, Joseph, I would have known you in hell, you look so much like your father."

These were her exact words, said Joseph F., and they made a deep impression upon him as well as giving him a shock at the manner in which they were spoken. She did not appear to recognize Samuel, although he had visited her only about two years before. The following account is Joseph F. Smith's story of this visit to Nauvoo:

When Joseph (son of Emma) conducted Samuel and myself to our chamber, he said on bidding us good night: "John L. (meaning John L. Smith), slept here a while ago and he had a dream. I have had several myself in this room, and I would like you to remember what you dream tonight and let me know." This was but a few weeks after his acceptance of the position he now occupies (i.e. as president of the Reorganized Church) at the hands of William Marks and others. He was feeling somewhat zealous and urged us not to go any further on our missions, but stop and reflect, etc. In the morning I asked Samuel if he had dreamed anything. He replied, "No." I then told him my dream as follows: I thought I was standing

Samuel H. B. Smith

on a large pine raft, moored at the foot of the street in the edge of the river, and was fishing with a hook and line, and I thought I pulled out the fish almost as fast as I could bait my hook. The water seemed clear, so that I could see into it at a great depth. I stood on the outer edge of the raft, which was large, filling the space opposite the street. Soon I dropped my hook as usual, and no sooner had it sunk below the surface than I saw a huge gar making directly for it. Fearing I would lose my hook, I drew it rapidly out, but the gar was so determined to nab it that he ran out of the water more than half the length of my arm in the vain endeavor to snap it. However, I saved my hook and line and carried away my fish. When I told Joseph my dream he made no reply and the subject dropped.

Joseph F. and Samuel H. B. were treated very kindly by their Aunt Emma while they remained in Nauvoo. They also visited the three sisters of the Prophet Joseph Smith who were living at or near Colchester, McDonough County, Illinois. At this place there were a few members of the Church and a meeting was held and the two young missionaries delivered inspirational talks to the people assembled, including their three aunts.

—Joseph F. Smith, *Life of Joseph F. Smith: Sixth President of The Church of Jesus Christ of Latter-day Saints* (Salt Lake City, UT: Deseret News Press, 1938), 197–198.

Nauvoo Temple, painting by David H. Smith, ca. 1868

Nancy J. Tharpe

WE COME TO THE YEAR 1869. At this time my brother John lived at Nauvoo.... I went to visit him as I wanted to see him and his family, also I had a desire to see Nauvoo and the temple which had cost such a sacrifice to build, but instead it was a ruin.

While there I called on sister Emma Smith Bidamon. As the Brighamites were telling such great stories about her, I wanted to see her and hear from her own lips the answers to the questions I asked her. First I asked her if she had seen that revelation which was claimed by Brigham Young that Joseph Smith had on polygamy. She looked surprised at my question, then said, "I never saw it." I said I heard that she had taken the fire tongs and picked it up and burned it. She said, "I never burned it, that is some of Brigham's lies that he made up. There never was such a revelation to my knowledge and as for burning it, I never did." Then I asked her why she married a man out of the church. She said, "I had my own reasons for so doing to protect my children." She said she was warned that there would be an attempt to steal Joseph.

We talked on various subjects; she was a pleasant lady to talk with, her words were yea and nay, and to the point.

She showed me the room that Joseph left the morning they took him to Carthage jail. As he had been in jail several times before she was in hopes he would return this time, she said, but when she went to his room, she knew then he would never come back alive. These things have been in my mind, other things I have forgotten, so I write what I remember.

Mr. Bidaman treated me kindly, he showed me around in the Mansion and one room I remember he took us in, myself and two sisters-in-law, a well-furnished room. Here he showed us some relics, then we went to dinner and after a few days more visit I returned home to Nebraska where my home has been mostly ever since.

—Nancy J. Tharpe, "Reminiscence of Sister N. J. Tharpe," *Journal of History*, 11 (January 1918): 119-120.

RECOLLECTIONS OF NAUVOO, 1872

Julius Chambers in the *Brooklyn Eagle*:

TO PROVE THAT polygamy was not the corner-stone of Mormonism, a Gentile banker at Salt Lake City tells me that the "Church of Latter Day Saints" never has grown so rapidly as since the action of Congress making the practice of polygamy a felony. This thoroughly observant and traveled man is warm in his defense of the Mormons, as a people. His dealings with them, financially, are large. The only reason he asks me to withhold his name is because he does not want to be open to an imputation of talking to secure patrons.

A Protestant church member himself, he sees many excellent features in the Mormon church of the present time.

The polygamous features of Mormonism were engrafted upon the church by Brigham Young. My authority for this statement is no less a person than the widow of Joseph Smith, founder of the sect and finder of the alleged tablets containing the "Book of Mormon."

Emma Smith Bidamon, ca. 1870s

To me it is a pretty bit of memory. Let us talk about it:

"In the summer of 1872 I was paddling down the Mississippi in a canoe, built for the trip at Troy, New York. At the nightfall of a July evening, after a long day's work, I saw on the Illinois shore, upon a fine bluff, a red brick building that indicated a town of more than village size. Making a landing, I climbed to the top of the plateau and learned that the building that had attracted my attention was the only hotel in the place. What was much more important, I was told that the town was Nauvoo, for six years (1840 to 1846) the seat of Mormonism.

"When I applied at the office for supper I was received by an elderly woman.

"My eye-memory of the face and the figure of the distinguished old lady is quite distinct. She was tall, for her sex; her hair was gray, not white, and was combed straight over her temples. Her face was thin; her nose lean, aquiline, and pointed. Her mouth was small, her chin was badly shaped and protruded, her eyes were very noticeable, although their color can not be recalled. They were gray or blue, in all likelihood. I also remember her hands, which were small and had well-cared-for nails. Of course, all these characteristics were not noticed the first meeting, but were the result of studious observation that evening and during an hour passed in her interesting company next morning—because I remained at Nauvoo for the night.

"This lady was the widow of Joseph Smith, only wife of the first prophet of Mormonism, killed at Carthage, not many miles distant. Smith was an editor, and his kind of religion he printed in his newspaper, the *Nauvoo Expositor* [*Times and Seasons*], did not suit the people of that part of Illinois.

"Mrs. Smith was a sincere believer in her Husband's faith, but she took the earliest occasion to say that she did not believe in polygamy. She denounced the practice as 'vile and infamous.' She said it had 'blighted and dishonored a beautiful doctrine that came direct from an angel of God, inscribed upon plates of gold.'

"The dear old woman put me to shame with her dignified forbearance when I asked if she ever had seen those plates, or the miraculous pair of spectacles, known in Mormon history as 'Urim and Thummim.' She had not; but they veritably existed. Had I seen the 'Tables of Stone' that Moses received? Did I doubt the miracles of the Savior? Faith was comprised in the accept-

Ceramic Mug, fragment, excavated from Mansion House Outhouse.

ance of things not seen, she said to me.

"We talked long into the evening, for this aged woman appeared glad to see even a boy from the great east, which to her mind embodied the activities of the western world. She asked me a thousand questions, many of which I could not answer; not because they required a knowledge of science, art, or literature to reply to them, but for the reason that they were along lines outside of my personal experience. She appeared to know very little about the literature of the time and to care nothing about it. I remember she had read several of Dickens' novels. But her waking hours were largely passed seated in a tall-backed rocking-chair, near the edge of the bluff, with her eyes fixed upon the majestic Mississippi before her; after darkness fell she turned her vision down the river, toward the flickering lights of Keokuk, on the Iowa shore.

"She was a picture of a fine woman, stranded on the Ice-shore of age, amid surroundings with which she was entirely out of sympathy and among people who did not appreciate her intellect or her innate refinement. I believe she had a husband about the place, a native to the soil; but the pride of living she felt was not as his spouse.

"What earthly honor and renown she claimed was solely as 'the widow of Joseph Smith, a sincere believer, a devout man, and a loving husband.' Thus did she speak of the dead Prophet to me.

"My last sight of this venerable woman occurred next forenoon as she stood upon the bluff in front of the red hotel and waved her hand when I headed for the center of the broad stream to get into deep water on the Keokuk rapids . . . ."

—"Recollections of Nauvoo," *Register and Leader*, (Des Moines, Iowa), 13 June 1907, reprinted in the *Herald*, 54 no. 25 (19 June 1907), 541-42.

Emma's Red Hotel—the Nauvoo House as modified by Lewis Bidamon.

William E. McLellin's Visit

ON SATURDAY, THE 28th of August [1847], we visited the fated city of Nauvoo, and put up at the Nauvoo House, which is excellently kept by Mrs. Emma Smith, the enterprising widow of Joseph Smith, deceased. I spent about twenty-four hours in the deserted, and yet partly populated city. I had many hours conversation with Mrs. Smith, and learned many particulars from her, relative to the history of her husband from her first acquaintance with him, until the time of his cruel death. Among many others, I asked her this question:—Have you any confidence in the Book of Mormon, and the work of the last days! Her answer was prompt—"I have all confidence in that spirit of intelligence by which the Book of Mormon was translated; and by which the revelations were given to the church in the beginning." Although a widow, I admired the order of her family circle.

—McLellin, "Our Apology—and Our Tours, *The Ensign of Liberty*, 1, No. 3 (December 1847): 34, 35.

Sketch of the City of Nauvoo, ca. 1847

Portraits *of* Joseph & Emma

Portraits of Joseph Smith Jr. and Emma Hale Smith by Sutcliffe Maudsley, 1842.

MANY NAUVOO visitors enquired about Joseph Smith Jr.'s physical appearance. Around 1842, church member Sutcliffe Maudsley, an English immigrant, painted profile portraits of the Joseph and Hyrum Smith families. Early church members were familiar with these depictions. The family, however, preferred a more naturally posed front view portrait that hung in the Nauvoo Mansion House.

Joseph's Front View Oil Portrait

DRAWING UPON family tradition, Israel A. Smith, a son of Joseph III, indicated:

Sometime about 1842, or 1844, an artist came to Nauvoo, Illinois, and painted two oil portraits, one of my grandfather, the other of my grandmother, Emma.

—*Saints' Herald*, 97, no. 24 (12 June 1950):568.

Portraits of Emma and Joseph Smith Jr., probably painted by David Rogers, 1842, Community of Christ International Headquarters Museum, Independence, Missouri.

Portrait Location

VIDA E. SMITH, Joseph's and Emma's granddaughter, recalled that prized family paintings once hung in the sitting-room located in the lower southeast corner of the Nauvoo Mansion House. She indicated:

"These were removed to the chamber above which was the private room of my grandfather and grandmother."

—Vida E. Smith, "A Historic Trio.—No. II," *Autumn Leaves*, 16, no. 4 (April 1903):152.

THIS LOCATION for family paintings seems to be confirmed in a letter by Samuel H. Smith's son, Samuel H. B., which recounted the following story about Joseph Smith III:

...one day he went upsta[i]rs to show some person's [sic] his Father's likeness and after they had all turned, and stepped out the door, he turned around toward the likeness and he saw his Father.

—Samuel Harrison Bailey Smith to George A. Smith, 11 July 1860, in Buddy Youngreen, "Sons of the Martyrs' Nauvoo Reunion," *BYU Studies*, 20 (Spring 1980):361.

Debault Portrait of Joseph

IN 1853, ARTIST CHARLES DeBault visited Nauvoo and obtained Emma's permission to create a crayon sketch from the front view oil painting of Joseph.

—John Henry Evans, Joseph Smith, An American Prophet (New York: Macmillan Company, 1933), frontispiece.

Joseph Smith Jr. by Charles DeBault, 1853, taken from the front view oil portrait.

Junius Wells Visit

JUNIUS F. WELLS CAME to Nauvoo seeking information on behalf of the LDS Church. Wells was the editor of the Utah-based Latter-day Saint youth periodical, *The Juvenile Instructor*, printed in Salt Lake City, Utah.

Wells wrote of his visit with Emma in the winter of 1875-76:

[She] entertained me very hospitably and showed me the painting [of Joseph], then hanging in her bedroom in the Nauvoo House. I asked her if it were a good likeness of the Prophet. She replied, "No, he could not have a good portrait—his countenance was changing all the time." I then asked her what he thought of it and she replied: "I can tell you that, for I asked him and he said: 'Emma, that is a nice painting of a silly boy, but it don't look much like a Prophet of the Lord!'"

—Junius F. Wells, "Portraits of Joseph Smith the Prophet," *The Juvenile Instructor*, 65 (February 1930): 79-80.

George F. A. Spiller

WRITING OF AN 1856 visit with Smith relatives in Illinois, LDS member George F. A. Spiller related:

I ACCOMPANIED Elder Samuel H. B. Smith in his visits to his relations and formed a very agreeable acquaintance with Mrs. Sophronia McClarie, Mrs. Catherine Salisbury and Mrs. Lucy Milliken, the three surviving sisters of Joseph the Prophet, also, with his four sons, Joseph, Frederick, Alexander, and David, likewise the widow of the Prophet, now Mrs. Bidamon . . . . I have never seen Joseph in the flesh but judging from portraits the features of Mrs. Milliken appears to me to be an excellent facsimile of Joseph's.

—*Journal History*, 8 December 1856.

Katharine Smith Salisbury, sister of Joseph Smith Jr.

Lucy Smith Milliken, sister of Joseph Smith Jr.

Emma *to* Mrs. Pilgrim

OLD TIME SAINTS also questioned Emma about Joseph Smith's life and activities. Around 1870, Emma received a letter from Mrs. Emma Pilgrim, a Saint in Independence, Missouri, who was curious about Joseph's method of translating the Book of Mormon. Emma responded in March 1870 and included current information about her family:

Nauvoo, March 27, 1870

MRS. PILGRIM:
I acknowledge the receit of a letter from you a long time ago, and will now try to answer it. I should have done so immediately if I had not been called away from home by Joseph, his oldest daughter [Emma] was very sick with the lung fever, and she was so anxious to see me that her father

sent for me when I got there Emma was better, her fever was checked but she was very weak, but I found my son Alexanders wife just taken with the same fever the day before I got there, and she grew worse for seven days before the fever abated. She was so very bad that Joseph telegraphed to Alexander who was then in Sanfrancisco Cal to come home, and he brought my son David home with him, who had been quite sick before they started for home, and I had to stay at Plano a week longer before Alex wife was well enough for me to leave her or David well enough to go home with me, but through God the sick all recovered, through the prayers of faith and the administrations of the ordinances, and good nursing, without being under the painfull nessity of caling on a physetion. When health was sufficiently restored, I started for my home in Nauvoo bringin David and Emma home with me.

Now I would not troubled you with this long detail of events, but I feel it is due to you, that you should know what was the cause of my long delay, and also that you may know that it has not been willfull neglect or a wicked indifference to the subject of your inquiry as I always feel a peculiar satisfaction in giving all the information on that subject that I can.

Now the first that my husband translated, was translated by the use of the Urim and Thummin and that was the part that Martin Harris lost after that he used a small stone, not exactly, black, but was rather a dark color. I cannot tell whether that account in the Times and Seasons is correct or not because some one stole all my books and I have none to refer to at present, if I can find one that has that account I will tell you what is true and what is not.

Now you will allow me to call you Sister Pilgrim as Joseph called you so, and please write to me again and let me know how you get along, and how Mr. Hedrick and Mr. McLelland [McLellin] manages with regard to the church, do they have any regular church organisation, or not, and what their morral and religious influence is among the people there.

May God bless you is the prayer of your sister in the gospel.
Emma Bidamon

—Emma Smith Bidamon, letter to Mrs. Emma Pilgrim,
27 March 1870, Emma Smith Papers, P4, f43,
Community of Christ Archives.

Joseph Smith's Revision *of the* Holy Scriptures

JOSEPH'S BIBLE revision manuscripts remained in Emma's possession until April 1866 when the Reorganized Church's Conference authorized publication of Joseph's "New Translation." W.W. Blair, William Marks, and Israel L. Rogers were appointed to confer with "Sister Emma Bidamon" to obtain the manuscripts for the purpose of publication. The RLDS Publication Committee was chaired by Joseph Smith III and included Bishop Israel L. Rogers and former printer in the early church, Ebenezer Robinson.

Emma agreed to their request, and soon Marietta (Hodges) Faulconer (later known as Marietta Walker) and Mark H. Forscutt had prepared a complete draft using the manuscripts and the Phinney [Marked] Bible for reference. This draft consisted of a 206-page continual text of the Old Testament and a 244-paged text of the New Testament.

After editing, the 1867 committee manuscript was sent to Westcott & Thompson, Stere-

New Translation Manuscript, as it appeared before conservation.

otypers, Philadelphia, Pennsylvania, for publication. Ebenezer Robinson supervised the printing arrangements. Five hundred bound volumes of the newly completed "Holy Scriptures" arrived at Plano, Kendall County, Illinois, on 7 December 1867, for distribution to subscribers.

This work has since come to be known as the "Inspired Version" by the Community of Christ. The Church of Jesus Christ of Latter-day Saints refers to it as the "Joseph Smith Translation."

Following the completion of the Inspired Version, Joseph III published a tribute in the pages of *The True Latter Day Saints'*

Herald to his mother's devoted care which had been instrumental in preserving the manuscripts. Upon seeing this tribute, Emma wrote to Joseph saying:

Dear Joseph [III]
... I looked in the *Herald* and found there the balance of your note, it is too good for me. I feel very unworthy of so many good and pressious tokens of respect, and allmost veneration, from you, my son, and your faithful and much respected brethren in the work of preparing the New Translation, God bless you and them, with the light of his holy spirit. Those lines in the Herald caused me to retrospect those years of mine portrayed in them and I find not one thing in them that I done which was not just simply my duty to do, and that too without stopping to anticipate any future rewards, so that the happiness I now am enjoying is all new and unexpected I am indeed truly thankfull that the translation is what the good and cincerely honest have looked for but there are some that are so blinded with their own self conceit that they will cavil tho the word may be so plain that a fool can understand.

—Emma Smith Bidamon, Letter to Joseph Smith III, Nauvoo, Illinois, February 2, 1866 [sic 1867], Emma Smith Papers, P4, f36, Community of Christ Archives.

Emma's Affection for the Manuscript

FOLLOWING publication of the 1867 edition, the RLDS Church retained the manuscript materials. In a letter to her son Joseph Smith III in 1867, Emma Smith Bidamon said:

My own dear Joseph . . . Now as it regards the M of the new translation if you wish to keep them you may do so, but if not I would like to have them. I have often thought the reason why our house did not burn down when it has been so often on fire was because of them, and I still feel there is a sacredness attached to them.

—Emma Smith Bidamon, Letter to Joseph Smith III, Nauvoo, Illinois, 2 December 1867, Emma Smith Papers, P4, f39, Community of Christ Archives.

Joseph III's RLDS Church Presidency *and* Polygamy

THOUGH repeatedly urged to accept the presidency of the RLDS Church, Joseph III felt that it was more appropriate to await his own spiritual experience as confirmation before accepting the appointment. That experience came in 1860. LDS Apostle W.W. Blair recorded the news in his journal soon after paying a visit to Emma and her family in Nauvoo:

> Monday, 19 March 1860
>
> **T**HIS EVENING Bro I[srael] L. Rogers called upon me to go with Bro Wm Marks & himself to Nauvoo in answer to a request from Joseph Smith who wrote to Bro Marks that he had determined to soon take his fathers place in the Priesthood and desires an interview with himself and such others as Bro Marks might select. We proceeded on Monday night to Burlington and on Tuesday by 4 P. M. reached Nauvoo by Steam Boat Aunt Letty. Joseph & Emma recd us very kindly. We expressed ourselves with regard to the work. On comparison there appeared to be little or no difference of sentiment, we staid with them til Wednesday at 10. A.M. Before leaving Joseph told us he should attend the conference at Amboy, and Emma would endeavor to also. After we by request of Joseph had Prayers we took leave of the family and crosst [sic] the River to Montrose.
> —W. W. Blair, Journal, 1859-60, P2, J1, Community of Christ Archives.

Joseph III Ordained

AFTER RECEIVING spiritual confirmation of his calling, Joseph III travelled with Emma to Amboy, Illinois, where he was ordained the prophet and president of the Reorganized Church on 6 April 1860.

Joseph III believed polygamy to be wrong. He also believed that his father was a good man and therefore could not have been responsible for the introduction of polygamy in Nauvoo during the 1840s. Drawing upon his early adulthood legal training, Joseph III collected and evaluated stories about Nauvoo polygamy. Because of Joseph III's strong belief that his father was innocent of polygamy's evils, the Reorganized Church adopted a strong tenet of anti-polygamy.

As the new president of the Reorganization, Joseph III felt motivated to reconcile his own understanding of his father's life with the perceptions of others. Joseph III launched a campaign to discover the facts about polygamy and to clear his father's name.

T HE FOLLOWING representation, by E. C. Briggs, influenced Joseph III's attitudes about polygamy:

Emma Smith the Elect Lady personaly [sic] told me she never saw or heard of the Revelation on polygamy until she saw it in print published in the Seer by Orson Pratt in Washington D. C. Also she said I never burnt a copy of it, or any revelation given threw [sic] my husband. And all the statements that I ever burnt it or any other revelation is a tissue of lies manufactured by Brigham Young.

—E. C. Briggs, Salt Lake City, Utah, Letter to Richard J. Hawkins, Scranton, Pennsylvania, 28 March 1908, P13, f952, Community of Christ Archives.

William E. McLellin

But not all stories Joseph III encountered affirmed that his father was innocence of polygamy. After denunciations of polygamy appeared in the RLDS *Saints' Herald*, Joseph III received the following letters from William E. McLellin, a former apostle in the early church.

Y OU WILL PROBABLY remember that I visited your Mother and family in 1847, and held a lengthy conversation with her, retired in the Mansion house in Nauvoo. I did not ask her to tell, but I told her some stories I had heard. And she told me whether I was properly informed.

—William E. McLellin, Letter to Joseph Smith III, Independence, Missouri, July and 8 September 1872, Miscellaneous Letters and Papers, P13, f213, Community of Christ Archives.

William McLellin also wrote:

IDO NOT WISH TO SAY hard things to You of your Father, but Joseph, if You will only go to your own dear Mother, she can tell You that he believed in Polygamy and practiced it long before his violent death! That he delivered a revelation sanctioning, regulating, and establishing it--and that he finally burned the Awful document before her eyes.

—William E. McLellin, Letter to Joseph Smith III, Linden, Michigan, 10 January 1861, Miscellaneous Letters and Papers, P13, f137, Community of Christ Archives.

Joseph III frequently encountered contradictory statements such as these from first-hand observers about the events at Nauvoo. However, this did not deter Joseph III from his course. He believed that his father's public denials and direct evidence from his mother Emma held precedence over any other statements, which Joseph III interpreted as hearsay.

Joseph III expressed his view concerning polygamy in a letter to A. W. Dennetts, of Chicago:

The claim I make for my father in regard to plural ... marriage is this: There is not a line in the standard books of the Church as left by my father at his death, which properly construed gives warrant, or sanction to the doctrine, or practice....

Joseph Smith, and Hyrum Smith his brother, denounced polygamy in February and April 1844, publicly, in the *Times and Seasons*, the official organ of the Church... No revelation commanding, or permitting polygamy was presented, or accepted by the Church from father during his lifetime. No claim is made by even the Utah Mormons that a revelation said to have been received by my father was published to the church until August 29th 1852....

This document so presented by Brigham Young is not properly accredited as a copy of the original, if there ever was an original, the only evidence being the statement of Pres. Young that "it was a copy" which had been in his possession, seen of none but himself, and those who should see it, the original having been "burned by a wicked, wicked woman" meaning my mother. My mother positively stated on many occasions, that she never saw such a document and never burned it.... From these facts set forth above I have insisted that it cannot be shown by good and sufficient proofs that my father had such revelation, or was the author of Mormon Polygamy.

—Joseph Smith III, Letter to Mr. A.W. Dennetts, 10 March 1876, Joseph Smith III Letter Press Book, P6, JSLB4, pages 237-44, Community of Christ Archives.

Joseph III to Barbour, 1878

THE FOLLOWING LETTER to J.J. Barbour again demonstrates Joseph III's position:

I have yet seen no evidence, from any source, that convinces me that my father had or received the Revelation on Polygamy, said to have been given in 1843; in fact, the more I examine it, the more completely am I convinced that he did not.... I fully believe that [1852] revelation to have been a fraud upon the saints [by Brigham Young], which has wrought mischief and ruin.

—Joseph Smith III, Letter to Bro. J.J. Barbour, 15 May 1878, Joseph Smith III Letter Press Book, P6, JSLB1, pages 371-72, Community of Christ Archives.

Emma's Last Illness

AS EMMA GREW ILL toward the end of her life, Joseph III renewed his determination to exonerate the memory of his father.

While sitting by his mother's bedside, Joseph III read Edward Tullidge's Utah edition of *Life of Joseph the Prophet*. Upon completion, Joseph wrote Tullidge indicating that he liked the book about his father.

I read your *Life of Joseph the Prophet*, quite carefully, while watching at my mother's bedside during her last days.... I think I rose from its perusal refreshed; and if possible, with a grander view of the mission of Mormonism.

—Joseph III, Letter to Edward W. Tullidge, 9 May 1879, Joseph Smith [III] Letter Book 2, P6, pages 184-85, Community of Christ Archives.

This was a pivotal point of personal revitalization in Joseph III's life, which was perhaps intensified by the severity of his mother's illness.

Joseph Smith III *to* James Cobb

Joseph Smith III's Account of Emma's Testimony on the Book of Mormon

Feb 14th 1879

JAS. T. COBB;

... Yours of the 9th inst is at hand opportunely. Thank you for the reading of A. S. Hayden's letter. I reenclose it to you. The missing link—that which connects Joseph Smith, with Rigdon as co-plotters in a bold work of deception—bothers him and you. The world will be thankful to you if you find it; and so will I. Why be so distressed, and why spend so much time and effort, over so tremendous transparent a fraud, so stupendous a folly, as you deem Mormonism to be? Why not leave it to the tender mercies of time that by patient waiting wears out folly, either stamps out or reclaims viciousness, and vindicates truth?

"What have You learned!" That which displaces the corner stone upon which the fabric you are trying to build, rests. Mrs. Emma Bidamon, formerly Emma Smith nee Hale, from whom visiting her residence at Nauvoo, I have just returned, (the 13th inst), informs me that she was married to Joseph Smith, my father, in South Bainbridge, by a Justice of the Peace, whose name she believes was Tarbiell or Tarbell; that she was married at the house, or office of the Squire by him and not by Sidney Rigdon, nor a Presbyterian clergyman. That she never saw, or knew any Sidney Rigdon until long after the Book of Mormon was translated, and she thinks, published. She wrote for Joseph Smith during the work of translating as did also Reuben Hale, her brother and O. Cowdery. That the larger part of this labor was done in her presence, and where she could see and Know what was being done; that during no part of it did Joseph Smith have

Sidney Rigdon — The Spaulding Theory proclaims that Rigdon was the author of the Book of Mormon.

any Mss, or Book of any Kind from which to read, or dictate except the metallic plates which she knows he had.

Every argument advanced by you in support of the theory, that Sidney Rigdon was the responsible "Black Pope," behind the throne moving upon the pliant will of Joseph Smith, it seems to me, is defeated by this plain statement. I need spend no time, rapidly as [it] flies, to refute any based upon that proposition.

My mother further states that she knew the Pratts before she knew Rigdon, and is quite positive that Joseph Smith became acquainted with him, through the Pratts, one or both. The precise date when she became acquainted with the Messrs. P. P. and O. Pratt, she does not state, but is certain of the fact, that acquaintance with them preceded one with S. Rigdon.

S. Rigdon may have been at Bainbridge in 1826; so may Napolean 3rd but that by no means proves more than an opportunity for an acquaintance between Joseph Smith and him, if it be showed that Joseph Smith was there at the time. My mother states that she went to Bainbridge to visit a family named Stowell, that my father found her there, that her folks being opposed

A page from Solomon Spaulding's novel, entitled "Manuscript Story"

to her union with my father, the latter taking advantage of an opportunity pled for an immediate marriage. Stowell seconded his persuasions and without any previous purpose, "thinking she would a little rather marry him than any other man she knew," she yielded, and proceeding to the Squires they were married.

Some other things learned by me during my visit, confirms me in the faith that there was no collusion between Joseph Smith and Sidney Rigdon....

Respectfully, J. Smith [III]

—Joseph Smith III, Letter to James T. Cobb, 14 February 1879, Joseph Smith III, Letterbook JSLB2, 85-88, Community of Christ Archives.

Emma's Last Testimony

Joseph III visited Emma at Nauvoo and asked detailed questions. This introduction and interview were published in the *Saints' Herald:*

Introduction

IN A CONVERSATION held in the Herald office during the early days of the present year, between Bishop Rogers, Elders W. W. Blair, H. A. Stebbins and a few others, leading minds in the Church, it was thought advisable to secure from Mother Bidamon, (Sister Emma Smith), her testimony upon certain points upon which various opinions existed; and to do this, it was decided to present to her a few prominent questions, which were penned and agreed upon, the answers to which might, so far as she was concerned, settle these differences of opinion. In accordance with this understanding the senior editor of the *Herald* visited Nauvoo, in February last [1879], arriving on the 4th and remaining until the 10th. Sister Emma answered the questions freely and in the presence of her husband, Major Lewis C. Bidamon, who was generally present in their sitting-room where the conversation took place. We were more particular in this because it had been frequently stated to us: "Ask your mother, she knows." "Why don't you ask your mother; she dare not deny these things." "You do not dare to ask your mother!"

Our thought was, that if we had lacked courage to ask her, because we feared the answers she might give, we would put aside that fear; and, whatever the worst might be, we would hear it. The result is given below; it having been decided to give the statements to the readers of the Herald, in view of the death of Sister Emma having occurred so soon after she made them, thus giving them the character of a last testimony.

It is intended to incorporate these questions and answers in the forthcoming history of the reorganization.

We apologized to our mother for putting the questions respecting polygamy and plural wives, as we felt we ought to do.

—Joseph Smith III, *Saints' Herald* 26, no. 19 (1 October 1879):289.

The Interview with Emma, 1879

QUESTION. Who performed the marriage ceremony for Joseph Smith and Emma Hale? When? Where?

Answer. I was married at South Bainbridge, New York; at the house of Squire Tarbell, by him, when I was in my 22d or 23d year.

We here suggested that Mother Smith's history gave the date of the marriage as January 18, 1827. To this she replied:

I think the date correct. My certificate of marriage was lost many years ago, in some of the marches we were forced to make.

In answer to a suggestion by us that she might mistake about who married father and herself; and that it was rumored that it was Sidney Rigdon, or a Presbyterian clergyman, she stated:

It was not Sidney Rigdon, for I did not see him for years after that. It was not a Presbyterian clergyman. I was visiting at Mr. Stowell's who lived in Bainbridge, and saw your father there. I had no intention of marrying when I left home; but, during my visit at Mr. Stowell's, your father visited me there. My folks were bitterly opposed to him; and, being importuned by your father, sided by Mr. Stowell, who urged me to marry him, and preferring to marry him [than] to any other man I knew, I consented. We went to Squire Tarbell's and were married. Afterward, when father found that I was married, he sent for us. The account in Mother Smith's history is substantially correct as to date and place. Your father bought your Uncle Jesse's [Hale] place, off father's farm, and we lived there until the Book of Mormon was translated; and I think published. I was not in Palmyra long.

Question. How many children did you lose, mother, before I was born?

Answer. There were three. I buried one in Pennsylvania, and a pair of twins in Ohio.

Question. Who were the twins that died?

Answer. They were not named.

Question. Who were the twins whom you took to raise?

Answer. I lost twins. Mrs. Murdock had twins and died. Brother Murdock came to me and asked me to take them, and I took the babes. Joseph died at 11 months. They were both sick when your father was mobbed. The mob who tarred and feathered him, left the door open when they went out with him, the child relapsed and died. Julia lived, though weaker than the boy.

Question. When did you first know Sidney Rigdon? Where?

Answer. I was residing at father Whitmer's when I first saw Sidney Rigdon. I think he came there.

Question. Was this before or after the publication of the Book of Mormon?

Answer. The Book of Mormon had been translated and published some time before. Parley P. Pratt had united with the Church before I knew Sidney Rigdon, or heard of him. At the time of Book of Mormon was translated there was no church organized, and Rigdon did not become acquainted with Joseph and me till after the Church was established in 1830. How long after that I do not know, but it was some time.

Question. Who were scribes for father when translating the Book of Mormon?

Answer. Myself, Oliver Cowdery, Martin Harris, and my brother Reuben Hale.

Question. Was Alva Hale one?

Answer. I think not. He may have written some; but if he did, I do not remember it.

Question. What about the revelation on polygamy? Did Joseph Smith have anything like it? What of spiritual wifery?

Answer. There was no revelation on either polygamy or spiritual wives. There were some rumors of something of the sort, of which I asked my husband. He assured me that all there was of it was, that, in a chat about plural wives, he had said, "Well, such a system might possibly be, if everybody was agreed to it, and would behave as they should; but they would not; and besides, it was contrary to the will of heaven."

No such thing as polygamy or spiritual wifery was taught, publicly or privately, before my husband's death, that I have now, or ever had any knowledge of.

Question. Did he not have other wives than yourself?

Answer. He had no other wife but me; nor did he to my knowledge ever have.

Question. Did he not hold marital relations with women other than yourself?

Answer. He did not have improper relations with any woman that ever came to my knowledge.

Question. Was there nothing about spiritual wives that you recollect?
Answer. At one time my husband came to me and asked me if I had heard certain rumors about spiritual marriages, or anything of the kind; and assured me that if I had, that they were without foundation; that there was no such doctrine, and never should be with his knowledge or consent. I know that he had no other wife or wives than myself, in any sense, either spiritual or otherwise.

Question. What of the truth of Mormonism?
Answer. I know Mormonism to be the truth; and believe the Church to have been established by divine direction. I have complete faith in it. In writing for your father I frequently wrote day after day, often sitting at the table close by him, he sitting with his face buried in his hat, with the stone in it, and dictating hour after hour with nothing between us.

Question. Had he not a book or manuscript from which he read, or dictated to you?
Answer. He had neither manuscript nor book to read from.

Question. Could he not have had, and you not know it?
Answer. If he had had anything of the kind he could not have concealed it from me.

Question. Are you sure that he had the plates at the time you were writing for him?
Answer. The plates often lay on the table without any attempt at concealment, wrapped in a small linen tablecloth, which I had given him to fold them in. I once felt of the plates, as they thus lay on the table, tracing their outline and shape. They seemed to be pliable like thick paper, and would rustle with a metallic sound when the edges were moved by the thumb, as one does sometimes thumb the edges of a book.

Question. Where did father and Oliver Cowdery write?
Answer. Oliver Cowdery and your father wrote in the room where I was at work.

**Question. Could not father have dictated the Book of Mormon to you, Oliver Cowdery and the others who wrote for him, after having first written it, or having first read it out of some book?

Answer. Joseph Smith [and for the first time she used his name direct, having usually used the words, "your father" or "my husband"] could neither write nor dictate a coherent and well-worded letter, let alone dictate a book like the Book of Mormon. And, though I was an active participant in the scenes that transpired, and was present during the translation of the plates, and had cognizance of things as they transpired, it is marvelous to me, "a marvel and a wonder," as much so as to anyone else.

Question. I should suppose that you would have uncovered the plates and examined them?

Answer. I did not attempt to handle the plates, other than I have told you, nor uncover them to look at them. I was satisfied that it was the work of God, and therefore did not feel it to be necessary to do so.

Question: Major Bidamon here suggested: Did Mr. Smith forbid your examining the plates?

Answer. I do not think he did. I knew that he had them, and was not specially curious about them. I moved them from place to place on the table, as it was necessary in doing my work.

Question. Mother, what is your belief about the authenticity, or origin, of the Book of Mormon?

Answer. My belief is that the Book of Mormon is of divine authenticity—I have not the slightest doubt of it. I am satisfied that no man could have dictated the writing of the manuscripts unless he was inspired; for, when acting as his scribe, your father would dictate to me hour after hour; and when returning after meals, or after interruptions, he could at once begin where he had left off, without either seeing the manuscript or having any portion of it read to him. This was a usual thing for him to do. It would have been improbable that a learned man could do this; and, for one so ignorant and unlearned as he was, it was simply impossible.

Question. What was the condition of feeling between you and father?

Answer. It was good.

Question. Were you in the habit of quarreling?

Answer. No. There was no necessity for any quarreling. He knew that I wished for nothing but what was right; and, as he wished for nothing else, we did not disagree.

He usually gave some heed to what I had to say. It was quite a grievous thing to many that I had any influence with him.

Question. What do you think of David Whitmer?
Answer. David Whitmer I believe to be an honest and truthful man. I think what he states may be relied on.

Question. It has been stated sometimes that you apostatized at father's death, and joined the Methodist Church. What do you say to this?
Answer. I have been called apostate; but I have never apostatized nor forsaken the faith I at first accepted; but was called so because I would not accept their new-fangled notion.

Question. By whom were you baptized? Do you remember?
Answer. I think by Oliver Cowdery, at Bainbridge.

Question. You say that you were married at South Bainbridge, and have used the word Bainbridge. Were they one and the same town?
Answer. No. There was Bainbridge and South Bainbridge; some distance apart, how far I don't know. I was in South Bainbridge.

These questions and the answers she had given to them were read to my mother by me, the day before my leaving Nauvoo for home, and were affirmed by her. Major Bidamon stated that he had frequently conversed with her on the subject of the translation of the Book of Mormon, and her present answers were substantially what she had always stated in regard to it.

—"Last Testimony of Sister Emma," *Saints' Herald* 26, no. 19 (1 October 1879):289-90.

THE

LATTER DAY SAINTS'

SELECTION OF

HYMNS.

PUBLISHED BY THE CHURCH OF JESUS CHRIST OF LATTER DAY SAINTS.

CINCINNATI, O.:
1861.

Emma's RLDS Hymnal, 1861.

Emma's Passing

As recounted by
Alexander H. Smith, 1879

Alexander H. Smith, ca. 1870s

WHEN I GOT TO Burlington, Iowa, I changed cars, ran down the river to Montrose and crossed over the river to Nauvoo. I went into the house as a boy, I felt like a boy coming home. I went in at the front door, and through the hall, and into the kitchen, where I knew my mother was usually to be found. My mother was not there. Another woman was there. I said to her, where is mother? Don't you know that your mother is sick? She is in the other room. I turned to go into the room, and as I opened the door and went into the room I saw my mother on the bed, and I had the testimony (that she was dying. I wished God would revive my) . . . mother, to let her remain with her children. I could not pray. I could not find words; I could not find voice; I could not find thought to pray. All was dark around me, and I labored in that agony for some time. Pretty soon the still, small voice of the spirit said, "If your mother dies she will be with her companion, Joseph; if she lives she cannot but live a few short years at most, of pain and anguish." And then the flood gates were let loose, and I said in my heart, "Father, it is enough, I will not murmur."

I went into the house, I found my step father; I said, Mr. Bidamon, are you not going to telegraph for Joseph? Oh no, your mother is not serious, she will soon be well. I did not listen to him. I sent a telegram to my brother Joseph, saying, "Joseph if you expect to see mother alive, come quick." In twenty six hours my brother was by her bedside. I asked him if he was surprised. "No," he said, "I have been waiting for that summons; I have been sleeping, as it were, with one foot out of bed, waiting for that summons."

I asked him how he knew, and why he was waiting for it. He said, "I had a vision. I saw my mother. She said to me, Come, Joseph, I will show you my home; and I went with her. She took me into a beautiful mansion; she showed me all through the mansion, all of its beauty and arrangement; one of the most beautiful mansions, he said, that one could conceive. And I noticed, too, Alexander, that careworn look that we always saw on our mother's face after father's death, was gone, and she looked young and fresh, and as though she was happy and glad. She said to me, 'Joseph, this is my home.' And he said he knew that Father would call her soon."

We waited upon my mother while she was sick. Just before she passed away she called, "Joseph, Joseph." I thought she meant my brother. He was in the room, and I spoke to him, and said, Joseph, mother wants you. I was at the head of the bed. My mother raised right up, lifted her left hand as high as she could raise it, and called, Joseph. I put my left arm under her shoulders, took her hand in mine, saying, Mother, what is it, laid her hand on her bosom, and she was dead; she had passed away.

And when I talked of her calling, Sr. Revel, who was with us during our sickness, said, Don't you understand that? No, I replied, I do not. Well, a short time before she died she had a vision which she related to me. She said that your father came to her and said to her, Emma, come with me, it is time for you to come with me. And as she related it she said, I put on my bonnet and my shawl and went with him; I did not think that it was anything unusual. I went with him into a mansion, a beautiful mansion, and he showed me through the different apartments of that beautiful mansion. And one room was the nursery. In that nursery was a babe in the cradle. She said, I knew my babe, my Don Carlos that was taken away from me. She sprang forward, caught the child up in her arms, and wept with joy over the child. When she recovered herself sufficient she turned to Joseph and said, Joseph, where are the rest of my children? He said to her. Emma, be patient.

And you shall have all of your children. Then she saw standing by his side a personage of light, even the Lord Jesus Christ.

Do you wonder why, as a son of that mother, I plead for those who believe upon the Lord Jesus Christ, and picture their beautiful home in the city of God, in the language that I do, when I realize that my mother occupies, or will occupy one of those beautiful mansions? It may be imagination; but it is grand; it fills me with a grand hope.

It enables me to see in the inspiration of God the light and glory and joy and happiness in the city and home of our God, where will dwell the ransomed on this earth, when it shall have been redeemed. May God bless you. Amen.

—Sermon by Alexander H. Smith, "Second Coming of Christ, the Home of the Redeemed," *Zion's Ensign* 19 (31 December 1908): 6, 7.

Emmas's Obituaries

DESERET NEWS.
Truth and Liberty.

No. 16.　　Salt Lake City,　　Wednesday, May 21, 1879.　　Vol. XXVIII.

DEATH OF EMMA SMITH.

The Utah *Deseret News* published the following items on May 21, 1879, after receiving news of Emma's death from the *Carthage Republican* of Hancock County, Illinois:

THE *CARTHAGE* (ILL.) *Republican* of the 7th inst., announces the death at Nauvoo, on the 30th April, of Mrs. Emma Bidamon, formerly the wife of the Prophet Joseph Smith; she was in the 76th year of her age.

This lady was the daughter of Isaac Hale, and was married to Joseph Smith the Prophet, at South Bainbridge, Chenango County, New York, on the 18th of January, 1827. The following particulars of her second marriage are clipped from the paper above named:

IN THE FINAL EXODUS of the Mormons from Nauvoo, in 1846, Mrs. Smith was not molested either by word or act, or her preference to a continued residence in city, questioned by anybody.

ON THE 23D OF December, 1847, Mrs. Emma Smith was united in marriage to Major L. C. Bidamon, by Rev. William Haney, a Methodist clergyman, as appears of record in the county clerk office in this city.

MAJOR AND MRS. Bidamon continued their residence in the Old Mansion House—formerly built and run as a hotel by Joseph Smith—until about ten ago, a brick structure on the river bank, which was partially built by the Mormon prophet in his lifetime, was completed and their residence changed to it.

TO THE OLD MEMBERS of this Church the deceased was well known, as a lady of more than ordinary intelligence and force of character. Her opposition to the doctrine of plural marriage which however she at first em-

73

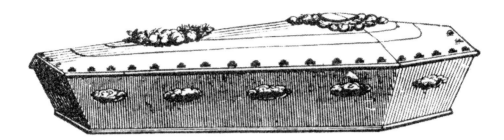

braced, led to her departure from the faith of the gospel as revealed through her martyred husband. She chose to remain at Nauvoo, when the Saints left for the West, and in consequence lost the honor and glory that might have crowned her brow as "the elect lady."

SHE WAS THE mother of four children, all the sons of the Prophet Joseph, viz. Joseph, now leader of the sect which commonly bears his name, Frederick, (deceased,) Alexander and David. It was mainly through her influence that they were led into the by-path wherein they have gone astray. She has now gone behind the vail [sic] to await the great day of accounts. There is no feeling of bitterness to the hearts of the Saints toward Sister Emma, but only of pity and sorrow for the course she pursued. May her remains rest in peace.

—Obituary of Emma Smith Bidamon, *Deseret News*, 21 May 1879.

Emma was buried near the lilac bushes.

The Saints' Herald

Official Paper of the Reorganized Church of Jesus Christ of Latter Day Saints.

"HEARKEN TO THE WORD OF THE LORD, FOR THERE SHALL NOT ANY MAN AMONG YOU HAVE SAVE IT BE ONE WIFE." — BOOK OF MORMON. JACOB 2:6.

Vol 26.   Plano, Ill. Wednesday, July 1, 1879   No. 13.

Notice of Emma's Death

SHE WAS THEN "the elect lady," and if so because of what she then was, she did right to remain in her then convictions, which she did.

So far as her being the responsible agent of leading her son Joseph, "the leader of the sect which commonly bears his name," astray, is concerned, we have this to state: We were of full age (and we believe of sound mind), when we made the choice that we did. Sister Emma did not use her influence to direct us into the way we chose. That she did approve of it, and gave it her hearty sanction, we admit, and revere her for it; while for the love of honorable deeds, pure life, and hatred of bigotry and oppression, either of dogma or person, that we may have inherited from her, we shall ever feel profoundly grateful. She has indeed "'gone behind the vail [sic],'" to answer to her account when called, and there those who now have "only pity and sorrow for the course she pursued," may find to their shame that "the elect lady" has not lost "honor and glory;" but that the dauntless and deathless spirit that burned within her when, widowed and bereaved, she dared to raise her voice against what she believed to be corrupting and destructive of purity and virtue in woman, will be crowned in celestial life and immortal peace.

We trust, so far as her oldest son is personally concerned, that those against whose principles we are at war, will cease casting the fault of our error and crime (if it be such), in choosing our fate in Mormonism upon her; so far as we can possibly do so, we absolve her from any and all responsibility in the matter, and desire that upon us alone may be visited the punishment due.

—*Saints' Herald* 26, no. 24 (July 1879):200.

Commentary

SISTER EMMA HAS been a singular rock of offense to Brigham Young and to his followers. Her straightforward opposition from which she never swerved, was at its beginning perilous, and afterwards, was evidently more provocative of anger than of pity in those whom she opposed. So far as Sister Emma's having first embraced the doctrine of plural marriage, from which she afterwards revolted, is concerned, she directly and positively denied having anything to do with it, and, as published elsewhere, placed her testimony on record, that she neither saw nor handled the so-called revelation on celestial marriage; and this she did notwithstanding the statement of President Brigham Young, that she burned the original. [See *RLDS History*, Volume 3:352, 355.] The fact that this woman maintained her character for truth and integrity to the close of her life, and won a name for good, with the respect of even the enemies of Mormonism, together with the fact that she openly avowed and always stoutly defended her faith in "the faith of the gospel as revealed through her martyred husband," is a sufficient denial of the statement made by the *News* that she "departed" from that faith. She did what she could to stay the tide of evil that was creeping over the church, and maintained by her testimony and life what she as president; Elizabeth Ann Whitney, Sarah M. Cleveland, counsellors; Eliza R. Snow, secretary; and Mary C. Miller, Lois Cutler, Thirza Cahoon, Ann Hunter, Jane Law, Sophia R. Marks, Polly Z. Johnson, Abigail Works, Catherine Petty, Sarah Higbee, Phebe Woodruff, Leonora Taylor, Sarah Hillman, Rosannah Marks, and Angeline Robinson, members of the "Ladies' Relief Society," of Nauvoo, testified to in a certificate published in the *Times and Seasons*, in October of the year 1842, at the close of an article on marriage, in which the existence of any other system of marriage than the one published in the book of Doctrine and Covenants is denied. (*Times and Seasons*, Volume 3:940.) The relief society there named is supposed to have been the original one, of which the "Ladies' Relief Society," of Salt Lake City, is the successor. One distinguishing difference between Sister Emma and some of the others who signed that certificate is, that she maintained her testimony by her subsequent life, while they did not.

—*RLDS History*, Volume 2:598.

Obituary from the *Nauvoo Independent*

MRS. EMMA BIDAMON, whose departure from this life on April 30, we noticed in our last issue, was the daughter of Isaac and Elizabeth Hale, and born in the town of Harmony, Susquehanna County, Pennsylvania, July 10, 1804. She remained an inmate of her father's house until January 18, 1827, when she married Joseph Smith, the founder of the Mormon Church, as it is usually termed. It is stated that Joseph Smith stole her away from her father's house and married her against the advice and wishes of her friends; but whether this is true or not, it appears that after her marriage, her father relented, as fathers usually do, and the runaways returned to her father's farm, where they remained for some two or three years. From there Mrs. Smith removed with her husband to Palmyra, New York, and from there to Kirtland, Ohio, where she was a constant participant in the busy scenes of the church's prosperity and exodus from there. During her stay at Kirtland, her two sons, Joseph and Frederick G. W., were born, of whom Frederick died in Nauvoo, in 1862. From Kirtland, Mrs. Smith went with others to Missouri, living with her husband, first in one county and then in another, till the mobbing in 1838; when, her husband having been taken prisoner and lodged in Liberty Jail, in Ray [Clay] County, she, with the great mass of the Mormons, was obliged to leave Caldwell County and the state of Missouri. She arrived at Quincy, Illinois, where she and other refugees from violence were kindly received. Here, some six months after his capture, Mrs. Smith was joined by her husband, he having escaped from the custody of his guards, in going from Liberty to another county ostensibly for trial, and not long afterwards, they settled on the Hugh White farm below Commerce, in the building now standing opposite the Riverside Mansion, on the west.

During the five years from their first settling here, Mrs. Smith bore her part in the toils, deprivations, and sickness incident to the settling of a new country. Her son Alexander, was born in her stay in Missouri, and one other, Don Carlos, was born to her in Nauvoo, but died in his infancy. Her husband, Mr. Smith, was killed at Carthage, June 27, 1844, and Mrs. Smith remained at Nauvoo during all the troubles attending the expulsion of the Mormons from the state of Illinois, except the time between September, 1846, and February, 1847, when she, with two or three families that went with her, sojourned at Fulton City, in Whiteside County, in this State. Her youngest son, David Hyrum, was born November 17, 1844, a few months after Mr. Smith's death.

Mrs. Smith was keeping the Nauvoo Mansion, so long the principal hotel of the place, during the year 1847, and here became acquainted with Major Lewis C. Bidamon, one of the new citizens, as they were called, and on December 27, 1847, she was married to him, the Reverend William Hana, brother to the celebrated Reverend Dick Hana, of the M. E. Church, officiating in the marriage ceremony.

Mrs. Bidamon raised her four boys and an adopted daughter, now Mrs. Julia Middleton, to woman and manhood, all of whom, except Frederick before named, now mourn her demise. She was the companion of her first husband for eighteen years, and shared his fortune during the fourteen years of his active ministry; passing through scenes of sorrow and trouble that tested her character to the extreme; and won the esteem of all. She was the wife of Major Bidamon from 1847 to 1879, nearly thirty-two years, and proved herself to be a worthy companion. She was mistress of the Nauvoo Mansion, with the exception of two or three short intervals, from its erection in 1843 till about 1871, when the building fell into the hands of her sons Alexander and David, when she and her husband removed to the Riverside Mansion in a part of what was known as the Nauvoo House, on the river-bank at the foot of Main Street. She was loved and respected by all her neighbors, for her charitable and kind disposition. She was a good and faithful wife, a kind and loving mother, as the expressions of her children and associates will verify. If such a record as she has left does not render a person worthy of a better life beyond, it is difficult to conceive how it can be done.

The body of Mrs. Bidamon was laid in the parlor of the Mansion, where she resided, in the morning after her demise, and in the evening of the same day, was placed in the burial case, where it was constantly watched by Mrs. Middleton, the inmates of the Major's house and a few intimate friends, until the afternoon of Friday, May 2. At twelve p.m., the friends and relatives of the deceased began to arrive, and at two p. m., the hour set for the services, the rooms were filled, and a large number in attendance could not find entrance, but stood gathered near the open doors to listen.

The funeral services were in charge of Elder John H. Lake, of Keokuk, Iowa; the sermon was delivered by Elder Joseph A. Crawford, of Burnside, this county; the singing was in charge of Elder Richard Lambert, of Rock Creek Township. There were six bearers, five of whom were nephews of Mrs. Bidamon, sons of sisters of Joseph Smith, her first husband....

After the services were over, the large company filed through the room past the coffin, viewing the face of the deceased as they passed. It was a touching sight to see those citizens so long acquainted with the silent sleeper, while she was living, pausing beside her to take a last look at her peaceful face, so calm amid the grief of the assembly. Now and then one to whom she had been dearer than to others, would caress the extended hand, or gently stooping lay the hand upon the cold face or forehead, some even kissing the pale cheek in an impulse of love and regret. But scenes of grief must pass—the family at length took leave of her whom they had so long known and loved. The coffin lid was put in place, the six bearers raised their burden reverently, and with the mourning train, passed to the place of interment, upon the premises of her oldest son, near by, where with solemn hymn and fervent prayer the remains were left to their long repose.

The assembly was large; almost every one knew Mrs. Bidamon, some intimately and for many years; some but for a few months, but it is safe to say that the respect, esteem, and love with which she was regarded by all, is but a just tribute to the sterling virtues of the woman, wife, and mother, whom the community so soberly, so sadly, and so tenderly laid away to rest, on that beautiful May day, by the side of the Father of Waters, the mighty Mississippi.

Mrs. Bidamon was a member of the Reorganized Church of Jesus Christ of Latter Day Saints, and her funeral services were conducted by elders and members of that body of believers, and the sermon was indicative of their hopes in the millennium yet to come.

At the close of the sermon, Elder Lake paid a touching tribute of love and respect to Mrs. Bidamon, in a few words expressive of her faith and hope, stated to him a few days before her death. Taken as a whole the funeral was remarkably impressive and tenderly sad.

—*Nauvoo Independent.*

 EMMA'S NAUVOO

Reflections of Emma

An obituary in the July 1879 *Women's Exponent*.

RS. EMMA BIDAMON, died in Nauvoo on the 30th of April [1879]. Among the Latter-day Saints, in days gone by, she was familiarly known as "Sister Emma," wife of the Prophet Joseph Smith. She was considered rather a remarkable woman, possessing great influence and unusually strong characteristics, which if properly directed, as in the early days of the Church, would have made her name illustrious in the history of the Latter-day Saints down to the end of time.

—*Women's Exponent* 7, no. 24 (July 1879):243.

Emma's Burial

Joseph Smith III reflected on his mother's burial in the Smith Family Cemetery:

We returned home on the 6th from Nauvoo, where we have been watching by the bedside of Mrs. Emma Bidamon, our loving and loved mother. We waited in watchful expectation for the end, which came at 4:20 in the morning of the 30th of April, when she breathed her life out gently, and slept the last sleep in peace. On Friday, May 2d, neighbors, friends and relatives, bore her remains to the place where our relations lie, and there we left them, where on her grave the gentle dew and genial sunshine, the storm and the calm, shall bless her repose until with them that sleep she shall rise to the eternal newness of everlasting life.

—Joseph Smith III, "Editorial Items," *Saints' Herald*, Vol. 26 (15 May 1879):152.

In the time following Emma's death, members of the Reorganized Church gathered to report remembrances of Emma and stories supportive of the church's position against polygamy.

David Holmes: Visit *with* Emma

David S. Holmes, ca. 1890

Joy, Ill., Rout[e] 3, Feb 28, 1915

BROTHER ELBERT A. Smith: I write you in regard to [the] testimony of Sister Emma Bidamon given in presence of Jacob Brown of Galesburg Ill James Vernon and wife and Viola V. Vernon Isaac B. Larue and D. S. Holmes June 20th 1863

We all were going to String Prairie Su [Sioux] Co. Iowa to a Special Conference so we spent the 20 visiting Nauvoo We met your father David H. Smith near the Mansion house and Bro Brown introduced us all to him and he took us to the old home Sr. Emma was well a[c]quainted with Brother Brown but had not met him Since 1844 after the introduction to all of us, he said to her, did Joseph Smith get the revelation on poligamy [sic] and in all the earnestness of her honest heart She said Joseph Smith was a true, loving husband as good a husband as any woman ever had and if he ever had another wife, I never knew it Then Bro. Brown asked her when she first saw the revelation and she said in September 1852. I am the only one left of this company of Buffalo Prairie Saints except Sister Viola V. Short and was 19 years old when [we visited Nauvoo] Nov 17 1863 [I] am now 70 years old and have treasured this Statement of your Gran[d]Mother as I now remember her earnest manner my heart well[s] up in love for this Elect Lady of the Latter Day Saints Church and I have told this story from [the] pulpit and to hundreds in private.... I live at Buffalo Prairie Ill. and have presided over this branch 27 years last April I hope to do some more good before [I] am called away.

Your Bro. in Bonds,
D. S. Holmes

—David S. Holmes, Joy, Illinois, Letter to Elbert A. Smith, 28 February 1915, P13, f1271, Community of Christ Archives.

Hudson Statement about Emma Hale Smith Bidamon

Testimony taken during a conversation of Lou Hudson with Garland E. Tickemyer on 21 July 1940, following a memorial service at the graves of the martyrs.

At the time Mr. Lewis L. Hudson was past 80 years of age and mentally alert. He was not affiliated with any church.

MY FATHER CAME here (Nauvoo) about 1850 I reckon. I was born here in 1860 and was well acquainted with the Smith family. Emma Smith Bidamon died when I was 18 years old. I knew Joseph Smith, Jr. [III], his wife, and three daughters—Emma, Carrie and Zadie. I was Joseph's agent for this place (the homestead).

When I was a boy I used to play down here at the Smith place with Fred A. Smith and Mrs. Bidaman's step-son, Charlie Bidaman. Why I was like one of the children—I ate half of my meals there and the things that I'm telling you I know are true. I've eaten many a cookie that Mrs. Bidaman cooked for us.

There never was a woman with a finer character than Emma Smith Bidaman. I never heard her say a cross word in my life. In fact, she never had much to say—she was just a nice stately woman to talk to. I never saw her even on the street out of that place. I have often heard her say that it positively was not true that Joseph Smith had any other wives.

Signed by Witness
G. E. Tickemyer

Jimison Statement about Emma Hale Smith Bidamon

Nauvoo, Illinois, August 29, 1940

TO WHOM IT MAY concern:

I was a near neighbor of Mrs. Emma Smith Bidamon during my boyhood days in Nauvoo. I was born in September of 1859 near Nebraska City in the Missouri River country. My parents brought me to Nauvoo when I was seven years old. They bought the house on the Flat now known as the William Marks home from a man named Redfield. We lived there about a block from the home of Mrs. Smith Bidamon during my boyhood.

I saw Mrs. Smith Bidamon at least once a day most of the time. The young people of the community were in the habit of gathering of evenings at the Bidamon home. Major Bidamon (her husband) liked to have young people around him. I can still taste Mrs. Smith Bidamon's cookies after all these years. Everyone in town liked them. I went to school with her grandson, Frederick A. Smith.

Mrs. Smith Bidamon was awfully nice. There wasn't a better woman in Nauvoo. She was a good soul, a good Christian woman. She was good to everyone. Everyone thought well of her. She was always busy, a great woman to work. She did a good job raising her children. Her boys, Joseph, Alexander, and David were good boys. She was good to Mr. Bidamon's son Charles.

I have no connection with or interest in the Latter Day Saints religion. I am a Roman Catholic in church affiliation. I joined that church about five years after my marriage. I am making this statement solely in the interest of establishing correct portrayal of Mrs. Smith Bidamon.

I was a steamboat pilot on the Mississippi during my working days. I secured my steamboat pilot's license in 1881. I ran the ferry between Nauvoo and Montrose nearly thirty yers since my parents brought me here.

The Nauvoo House was built during my boyhood by Major Bidamon. I helped clean brick when the bricks were torn off the north end of the foundation. The building started there in the 1840's was not built far enough for anyone to use as a residence till my time. There was no roof on it, no floors in it.

(Signed) Joseph S. Jemison

—Statements about Emma Hale Smith Bidamon, circa 1940, Biographical Folder Collection, P21, f73, Community of Christ Archives.

Nauvoo House, painting by David H. Smith. Courtesy Lynn Smith Family.

Lewis Bidamon's Passing

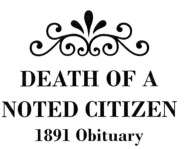

DEATH OF A NOTED CITIZEN
1891 Obituary
Nauvoo Independent

Major Lewis Crum Bidamon, ca. 1860s.

WEDNESDAY morning at 8 o'clock occurred the death of Major L. C. Bidamon, after a lingering illness of three years. He suffered from no disease whatever, simply a wearing out of vital forces, a natural result of old age. Mr. Bidamon has been near death's door for the past year or more and therefore his death was not an unexpected surprise to our citizens.

By his death passes away one of our pioneer citizens, a quaint and well-known character of Mormon times.

Mr. Bidamon was born at Williamsport, W. Va., on Jan. 16, 1806, and therefore was 85 years and 25 days old. He was a resident of Fulton county during the early Mormon troubles of this county. He was a lieutenant colonel of the 32nd Regiment of Illinois Infantry, and moved to Nauvoo in 1846 and thence took an active part among the new citizens in the existing difficulties.

He was more widely known perhaps on the account of marrying Mrs. Emma Smith, the widow of the great Mormon prophet, Jos. Smith, shortly after the exodus of the Mormons, and joined her in keeping the Mansion House, which they conducted for years and which was the chief hotel in the city. His wife died in 1878 and some time later he was married to Mrs. Abracrombie [Abercrombie], who survives him as also do two children, Mrs. M. E. Gibson of Chicago, and Chas. E. Bidamon of Nauvoo; and a sister and a brother, Mrs. J. M. White of Chicago and John C. Bidamon of San Luis Obispo, California.

Deceased was probably the best known man in the city. He became widely known to the general public as the husband of Joseph Smith's widow and the visits of all noted people, newspaper correspondents, authors, etc., was never complete without paying a visit to the Major and the old Mansion House; and all writers' accounts of Nauvoo invariably gave an elaborate write up of him. He was good-natured, humorous and a jocular character and he scarcely left a visitor go without first "selling" him on his "red bat" and "dark closet" jokes—jokes that have become famous. He was always spry and healthful until three years ago when he slowly began to fail, and finally succumbed to the inevitable.

The funeral was held Sunday afternoon, Feb. 15, in the burial lot on the homestead grounds, beside the grave of his wife, Emma Smith.

—Lewis Crum Bidamon, obituary, *Nauvoo Independent*, February 13, 1891, Emma Smith Papers, P4, f46, Community of Christ Archives.

IN A SKETCH OF HIS mother's life, Joseph Smith III wrote that her second husband's habit of excessive drinking sometimes rendered their life unpleasant:

It is to the credit of Mrs. Bidamon's stability and excellent qualities of government and parental control, that she managed to keep her boys from contracting the same evil habit.

—Joseph Smith III, untitled biographical Sketch of Emma Hale Smith Bidamon, P13, f2302, Community of Christ Archives, p. 22.

However, Emma did not completely succeed in her efforts to keep her oldest son from emulating his step-father's use of tobacco. In later years Joseph III wrote to Thomas Jacobs:

I send by this mail a small box containing a pipe and a bit of good tobacco for you. I once loved a pipe, and know what a solace to worry it sometimes is to sit down and enjoy a good pipe ....

—Joseph Smith III to "Friend Jacobs," 9 June 1881, JSLB1A, 224, Community of Christ Archives.

Inez Smith Davis

Correspondence between Alexander H. Smith's daughter, Inez, and Joseph III's daughter, Audentia Smith Anderson, describes the locations of Smith Family graves:

Independence, Missouri,
June 30, 1930

DEAR COUSIN Audentia: I had your interesting letter some time ago, and the other day had one from Joseph F. Smith, Jr. of Salt Lake City, whom I had approached with some trepidation concerning the Family Cemetery. However, I will say this, that he has always been very kind in answering all my inquiries up to the present, and I think in this case has given me the key to the whole situation in regard to those buried in the cemetery. He admits his information is very vague, almost traditional in fact, but it sounds probable, and more over what reason would he have in this case to misrepresent facts? He says,

"In relation to the burial places of the members of the Smith family in Nauvoo, I am forced to say our information is very meager. There is little in the records telling us where burials took place, such a thing being considered of little importance by those who wrote. There are accounts of deaths and funerals but the burial grounds are not mentioned. However the best information we have is to the effect that grandfather Joseph Smith, the patriarch, and Don Carlos were buried in the cemetery southeast of the Temple, where burials in the early days of Nauvoo took place. There are two cemeteries outside of the family lot. Samuel Harrison and Caroline Grant Smith (wife of William) were buried in the family plot.

When the Icarians came to Nauvoo, after the exodus the flats east of Nauvoo were converted into vineyards and the bodies in the cemetery were moved to another place. Among the bodies removed was that of Jennetta Richards, etc. . . . It is our understanding, though the information I have is rather vague, that the bodies of grandfather Joseph Smith, Don Carlos, Robert B. Thompson (Joseph Smith's secretary) and some others were moved to the family burial ground about 1846, before the exodus was completed."

I really believe that between this and Uncle Joseph's *Memoirs*, we have the facts. Probably the first burials were the secret burials of the martyrs. Then when Nauvoo was evacuated, the bodies of relatives were moved to the family plot, placed somewhere near this secret spot. Naturally Emma Smith would not see this burial ground plowed up for a vineyard and not have these bodies moved, including that of her 14-month old child "Don Carlos" to a place where she knew they would be safe from the invaders, i.e. her own private property?

Mother remembers the grave of Frederick G. W. and says she could go right to the spot, as she often remembers going with her grandmother and putting flowers upon it. I hope for an opportunity to take her there. She says as a child she remembers there were "many graves." I have never discussed the matter with Emma J., but I will. Her memory has proven remarkably accurate on many points. She also lived with Emma Hale a part of the time when she was about twelve to fifteen and had Uncle David as a companion in those days.

It is rather pleasant looking up these things. When Cousin Fred asked me about the graves, I only knew of the three, Joseph, Hyrum, and Emma and Emmeline G. Smith her two children and the Gifford grave. It is wonderful what can be found even yet without very much effort, isn't it? How I wish we had started to inquire years ago . . .

—Inez Smith Davis, letter to Audentia Anderson, 30 June 1930, P23, f178, Community of Christ Archives

THE FAMILY erected Emma's memorial in 1891. Joseph III enlisted Lewis L. Hudson, a local Nauvoo storekeeper, to supervise the project. Hudson "knew Mrs. Emma Smith Bidamon for many years and as a friend of the family was well acquainted with her, having been at her home many times." The completed monument, costing about $30.00, consisted of a large horizontal tombstone supported by a brick base.

—Emma Smith Bidamon Biographical Folder, P21, f73; Hudson to Joseph Smith III, 2 June 1891, Joseph Smith III Papers, P15, f17, item 14, Community of Christ Archives.

Smith Family Burial Ground

IN 1927, JOSEPH SMITH Jr.'s, Hyrum Smith's, and Emma Smith Bidamon's remains were identified and subsequently re-interred in the Smith Family Burial Ground next to the Homestead in Nauvoo, Illinois.

Even before the death of Joseph Smith Jr., the family set apart a portion of their land for the burial of family members and close friends. Subsequent research includes the following individuals in the burial ground. There are about 24 Smith family members in all. The Smith Family Cemetery is administered by the Community of Christ Historic Sites. Visitors are welcome.

Emma's Grave, Nauvoo, Illinois, Joseph Smith III, Heman C. Smith, Edmund L. Kelley, George Lambert, Alexander H. Smith.

SMITH FAMILY BURIAL GROUND, NAUVOO, ILLINOIS

Generations are indented.   *Indicates probably buried here.

Joseph Smith Sr., *1771-1840*
Lucy Mack Smith, *1775-1856*

- Hyrum Smith, *1800-44*
  - Hyrum Smith Jr., *1834-41*
- Joseph Smith Jr., *1805-44*
  Emma Hale Smith Bidamon, *1804-79*
  - Frederick Granger Williams Smith, *1836-62*
  - Don Carlos Smith, *1840-41*
  - stillborn son, *1842*
    Emmeline Griswold Smith (JS III's wife), *1838-69*
    - Evelyn R. Smith (JS III's daughter), *1859*
    - Joseph Arthur Smith (JS III's son), *1865-66*
- Samuel Harrison Smith, *1808-44*
  Mary Bailey Smith, *1808-41*
  - Lucy B. Smith,* *1841*
- Don Carlos Smith, *1816-41*
  - Sophronia C. Smith, *1838-43*

Caroline Grant Smith* (William Smith's wife), *1816-41*

Others:
Lewis Crum Bidamon, *1806-91*
Celeste Gifford, *1855-56*
Edwin James Gifford, *1863-65*
Maude A. Gifford, *1871*
Wilber W. Gifford, *1853*
Robert B. Thompson,* *1811-41*

Other Resources *About* Emma

Sketch of Emma Smith by David Hyrum Smith, ca. 1860s.

Linda King Newell and Valeen Tippets Avery, *Mormon Enigma: Emma Hale Smith*, 2nd ed., Urbana: University of Illinois Press, 1994, paperback, 394 pages. [Award-winning biography.]

Valeen Avery, "Emma Smith: An Unknown Sister," in Maren M. Mouritsen, ed., *Blueprints for Living: Perspectives for Latter-day Saint Women*, Volume 2, Provo, UT: Brigham Young University Press, 1980.

Valeen Avery, "Emma Smith Through Her Writings" *Dialogue: A Journal of Mormon Thought* 17, no. 3 (Autumn 1984):101-06.

Valeen Avery, *From Mission to Madness: Last Son of the Mormon Prophet*, Urbana: University of Illinois Press, 1998.

Valeen Avery, "The Last Years of the Prophet's Wife: Emma Hale Smith Bidamon and the Establishment of the Reorganized Church of Jesus Christ of Latter Day Saints," M.A. thesis, Northern Arizona University, 1981.

Valeen Avery and Linda King Newell, "Lewis C. Bidamon, Stepchild of Mormondom," *BYU Studies* 19, no. 3 (Spring 1979):375-88.

Valeen Avery and Linda King Newell, "New Light on the *Sun:* Emma Smith and the *New York Sun Letter,*" *Journal of Mormon History* 6 (1979):23-25.

Valeen Avery and Linda King Newell, "Sweet Counsel and Seas of Tribulation: The Religious Life of the Women in Kirtland,"

BYU Studies 20, no. 2 (Winter 1980):151-62.

Valeen Avery and Linda King Newell, "The Elect Lady: Emma Hale Smith" *Ensign* 9, no. 9 (September 1979):64-68.

Valeen Avery and Linda King Newell, "The Lion and the Lady: Brigham Young and Emma Smith," *Utah Historical Quarterly* 48, no. 1 (Winter 1980). Reprinted in Roger D. Launius and John E. Hallwas, eds., *Kingdom on the Mississippi Revisited.*, Urbana: University of Illinois Press, 1996, 198-213.

Valeen Avery, Linda King Newell, and Maureen Ursenback Beecher, "Emma and Eliza and the Stairs," *BYU Studies* 22, no. 1 (Winter 1982):87-95.

Paul Ludy, *Visits to Old Nauvoo*. Three visitors describe Nauvoo — a Methodist minister in 1843, an English illustrator in 1853, and an RLDS writer in 1909. 28 pages.

Youngreen, Buddy. *Reflections of Emma, Joseph Smith's Wife* (Orem, UT: Grandin Book, 1982).

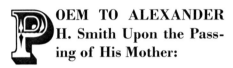

POEM TO ALEXANDER H. Smith Upon the Passing of His Mother:

Weep not brother, no despairing,
Grieving now should rend thy breast;
Out beyond the night of sorrow,
Dawns a beautiful to-morrow;
While through the rifted clouds appearing,
Breaks the morn of endless rest;
That awaits thy darling mother,
Passed to Paradise, before,
Where no pain or trouble, brother,
E're will cross her pathway more.

Grand has been her mission,
   Living.
When the gospel sun-burst come;
Side by side with Joseph bearing
Up the standard. Gladly sharing
All the trials; calmly giving
For the gospel, friends and home.
Pressing onward, faltering never;
Though thy father in the strife
Died a martyr, crossed death's river,
To the golden port of life.

God be praised, thy aged mother
Did not pass behind the veil;
'Till she heard the proclamation,
Ushering in the restoration.

—Joseph Crawford, 10 May 1879, *Herald* 27 (June 1879):180.

Printed in the United States
203296BV00003B/262-345/A